A Second Look at the Savior

Hearing His Voice

BYRON SMITH

WESTBOW
PRESS®
A DIVISION OF THOMAS NELSON
& ZONDERVAN

Scripture taken from the NEW AMERICAN STANDARD BIBLE®, Copyright © 1960,1962,1963,1968,1971,1972,1973,1975,1977,199 5 by The Lockman Foundation. Used by permission."

WestBow Press books may be ordered through booksellers or by contacting:

WestBow Press
A Division of Thomas Nelson & Zondervan
1663 Liberty Drive
Bloomington, IN 47403
www.westbowpress.com
1 (866) 928-1240

ISBN: 978-1-5127-7389-7 (sc)
ISBN: 978-1-5127-7391-0 (hc)
ISBN: 978-1-5127-7390-3 (e)

Library of Congress Control Number: 2017901759

Print information available on the last page.

WestBow Press rev. date: 08/31/2017

Contents

Part 4 'Pressing Forward in Stillness'

Part 5 'Closing Thoughts'

Contents

Part 4 *'Pressing Forward in Stillness'*

Part 5 *'Closing Thoughts'*

Introduction

Seek and find: it's the advice given by half of our friends and loved ones when we are in the midst of challenging times. *"Pray and prepare to move." "You need to play offensively." "Push forward and trust God."* It's the call to march forward to the River Jordan, and when the soles of your feet touch the water, God is going to make a path through the center of it.

Be still and know: it's what the other half of our friends and family will advise. *"Stop, listen, and wait in prayer." "Get off the field and out of the way." "Be still and let God work it out."* It's the call to stand strong where you are and wait even as you are tossed into the fiery furnace with Shadrach, Meshach, and Abednego.

Two classic ways to trust God, yet they are opposite once we move past prayer. So how do you know which path to follow? How do you know when God expects you to move or stand still? I believe we all struggle with this fork in the road at times, and learning how to see God's lead during these moments can give assurance we are on the right path.

A Second Look at the Savior: Hearing His Voice is a book that deals with finding and understanding God's will in our lives, especially in moments of pain and suffering. Our current society is ingrained in a very self-indulgent lifestyle. Rediscovering how to hear God's voice over our own expectations is vital to those trying to live the Christian life.

This book cannot answer every reader's questions or give exact answers to each situation. It can, however, teach us how to listen more closely to our Father in the midst of life storms. He boldly challenges us to move, and sometimes He is silent, and yet there are often things we don't see because the storms are so thick. If you want to see God's lead more clearly in your life and find a more intimate walk with Him, I truly hope you read this book. It was written for you.

Acknowledgements

First and foremost I would like to thank God for His time and patience while teaching me these lessons. This book is my gift to Him. I pray He uses it as He sees fit. A special thanks to Maryetta Holcomb for so much pre-editing help and advice. To Marshall Underwood, David Sargent, Ken Kilpatrick, Tracy Fryfogle, Donna Dungan, and Terry Cagle for time spent helping me fine tune ideas and thoughts. I want to thank so many others that have allowed God to work through them and in doing so impacting my life and this book.

To My Family
Autumn and Caleb, I hope one day this can be an encouragement to you and your children. I know at the moment you are too young to see the depths of these topics and lessons, but some day you will. To many nephews and nieces that I'm not in touch with often because of location and work: I hope this book can benefit you as well. Each of you is in my prayers

often, and I know God will draw close to you because I've asked Him to. Please draw close to Him.

To My Wife, Jessica Smith
One of hardest thoughts I've tried to convey is my thankfulness for you. There are too many ways you've blessed my life to try to list them. I know there are many sacrifices made by the spouses of those in ministry. Thank you for not just making those sacrifices but encouraging them. Thank you for challenging me to never be satisfied with what we have done and always pushing me to pursue what could be.

'Foundational'

The fear of the LORD is the beginning of
knowledge;
Fools despise wisdom and instruction.
—Proverbs 1:7

But the voice of truth tells me a different story
The voice of truth says, "Do not be afraid!"
And the voice of truth says, "This is for My
glory"
Out of all the voices calling out to me
I will choose to listen and believe the voice of
truth.
—Casting Crowns

We must all face the choice between what is
right and what is easy.
—Albus Dumbledore

Chapter 1

The Question

"Whose voice are you listening to?"

"Seek and find" or "Be still and know." These different paths are presented so often in life, and knowing which one to follow isn't always as clear as we would like. Sometimes I wish God would put up heavenly road signs with flashing neon lights: "This way to avoid a ten-year financial setback." It may be that there are signs, but they are lost and jumbled, hidden among thousands of man-made signs that clutter the road. How do we know which choices to make? Which path do we take when the road forks? If God would just point which direction to proceed, I would move without hesitation. As I look back over the years, I see many of these moments when I had to choose, and I knew those choices would affect my life forever. I hope this book helps shine some light on the choices you have before you, but please do me this favor before we start: pray.

Pray every time you start a chapter. Pray when you're not reading at all. What we are dealing with is a communication process with the Father. Often it feels like an emotional roller coaster. One week you may think, *'I should do this'*, and the next, *'What was I thinking?'* Trying to have faith that God will give you direction isn't worth much if you aren't talking with Him. So talk to Him, and then listen.

As we begin, we need to make sure we are on the same page. I remember talking to a young man in high school who was ready to end his life and had already given suicide a feeble attempt. He was angry with God, or maybe more frustrated than anything else. The more he tapped God on the shoulder and asked Him where they were going, the harder it became to see the path. As I listened to him talk, I began to understand the way he viewed God. The longer he talked, the more I wondered what God he was talking about.

Some people want to make choices based on feelings. I'm sure you've heard the statement a time or two: "I just feel it in my heart that this is the right thing to do." I've also seen the outcome of those feelings. Sometimes it all works out, and sometimes it leaves us stranded in despair.

> **The heart is more deceitful than all else and is desperately sick; Who can understand it?**
> —Jeremiah 17:9

This verse describes the human heart as deceitful or misleading. Is this the guide we need to follow? People often do. Consider this scenario. There are a dozen individuals who all believe differently about who God is — Jehovah, Buddha, Brahma, or maybe Mother Earth. We could bring the sun god Ra back from Egyptian mythology or even Zeus from ancient Greece. Now ask them all, "Are you serving the true God?" What would they say? Each one would reply yes, and to prove it, many times they make this statement: "I know because I feel it in my heart." Let's push pause for a moment there and explore another thought. Please allow the preacher side to come out a little. If you follow this first chapter closely, a lot of things will come together. This foundation is necessary and will allow a more enjoyable read throughout the rest of the book.

Consider this passage:

> The serpent said to the woman, "You surely will not
> die! For God knows that in the day you eat from it your
> eyes will be opened, and you will be like God, knowing
> good and evil."
>
> —Genesis 3:4,5

This passage always bothered me just a little bit. It bothered me because of the angle in which Satan tempted them. Notice the bait? "...*you will be like God*" Isn't that every Christian's goal? It's our duty and promise to Christ when we choose to follow Him. Even the word *Christian* means "Christ like." You see, Eve and Adam were victims of their innocence ... or so I thought. The original words and their exact translations are as follows:

הְיִיתֶם you shall be וּכֵאלֹהִים as gods (Ref 1:1)

That sounds a little rigid, so I decided to look up other passages where these two words were translated. I found two.

> But you (king of Babylon) said in your heart, I will
> ascend to heaven; I will raise my throne above the stars
> of God, And I will sit on the mount of assembly in the
> recesses of the north. I will ascend above the heights
> of the clouds; I will make myself like the Most High.
>
> —Isaiah 14:13, 14

Those words are being translated in the section, "I will make myself like the Most High." They don't sound so innocent here. Again, in Ezekiel 28:2, it says,

> Son of man, say to the leader of Tyre, "Thus says the
> Lord God, Because your heart is filled up and you have
> said, 'I am a god, I sit in the seats of gods in the heart
> of the seas.' Yet you are a man and not God"

Here the translation is unmistakable. Saying, "I am a god", shows the intentions of the heart. Satan's angle in the garden wasn't promising them to be more like God: it was tempting them to be godlike. To become God, or at least His equal, was what baited the hook, and Eve wanted that. Adam then followed, and humanity fell because of pride.

Pride is as old as time itself, the mother of all sins. Proverbs 6:16 puts it as number one on God's "Top Six Things I Hate Most" list. Pride has been a problem for the saved and the lost, saints and sinners. It is the thought pattern that ultimately brings us to conclude that we know better than God. Sometimes it presents itself as "I need to help God out because He can't make it work."

As we look through scriptures and study the great heroes of faith, we find all have fallen victim to this mind-set. Abraham was promised a son, but after years of waiting he decided to help God. In taking Hagar as a wife, he fixed the "descendant" issue. We will talk more about him later. Aaron sat at the foot of Mount Sinai, waiting for Moses to return, and he decided to play God by making a golden calf. He claimed, "The people were angry, and I had to do something." Moses couldn't believe what had happened, yet later on we find him striking a rock in anger and crying out to Israel, "Must we bring you water?!" (Numbers 20:10).

The book of I Samuel nails the topic of pride in chapter 8. Israel "demands" a king. In verse 7 God tells Samuel to listen to the people and give them what they desire. They had not rejected Samuel as a prophet and leader; instead they had rejected God as their king.

Sometimes we miss pride at the heart of these problems because we sympathize with the people. Later, King Saul decided to offer up sacrifices, although it was not his place to do so. But listen to his reasoning: "We are on the verge of war, Lord. Your prophet wasn't here and something had to be done. You did make me king for a reason right? I just figured someone had to do it, and who better than your anointed."

It's David, angry with God's wrath on Uzzah. It's Jonah, angry at God's mercy on Nineveh. Time and time again the story repeats itself. People can't stand to pass up the chance to put on Jehovah's shoes and play god. The movie *Bruce Almighty* really hits home, doesn't it? The bottom line is that we think we know better than God in certain situations. You know, like the ones we are in. And so we rewrite God's playbook just a little. We reinvent God a bit more in our image.

This brings us to a term I want to look at: *universalism*. I never heard this term when I was growing up in the eighties or attending college in the nineties, but in the last few years the word has been used to define American society. Universalism basically states, "Just because someone doesn't believe in the God of the Bible doesn't mean he or she is wrong. As long as that person is trying to do what he or she feels is right, then that individual is okay." At first glance it's a really nice thought, but stay with me.

Universalism would say homosexuality isn't a sin; it's a preference. We can choose our sexual preferences, and please don't think it will stop with homosexuality. Smoking weed/pot isn't morally wrong; it's just modern. It should be legalized. Many states are doing exactly that. Abortion isn't murder; it's a choice. Do you realize that within this country our court systems have convicted people on involuntary manslaughter in cases where expectant mothers were attacked and lost the child? Yet at the same time a different mother in a different court is cleared of any charges brought against her by the father of the unborn child she aborted. How is it that our court systems say on one day it's a life and on another it's not? Simple, because in one case the mother wanted it to be a life and in the other she didn't. Universalism runs deep in this nation, and we have to acknowledge this.

Even some of our religious leaders have claimed that the Bible is outdated. So what are they implying? They have implied, "We should update it so God's Word fits us better."

Universalism is a system that says, "Be true to yourself." It pushes the idea that you can believe whatever you want to believe; just don't be convicted enough to tell someone else they should believe it. In this system you decide what is right and what is wrong.

The questions I'm dying to ask should already be on the tip of your tongue. If I am the one who decides what is right and wrong in my own life, who is my god? I am. Go back and quickly read all those statements within the first few pages and see if they don't sound like the world in which we live.

In short, the greatest nation on earth is falling for the first lie Satan ever told: הְיִיתֶם you shall be וּכֵאלֹהִים as gods.

I have seen Christians often look at passages they don't like and dismiss them—passages on sins or a verse that has to do with salvation that differs from what they believe. They defend their position: "I really don't see it that way; I feel that …" Do you see what happened there? Some are even so bold as to say, "I don't believe that verse or teaching" Why? Because it doesn't *feel* right to them; they *feel* differently on the matter. I stopped putting faith in what I felt a long time ago. I simply got tired of the emotional ride.

As you begin this study on hearing the voice of God in your life, please take some time to define who you are calling God. This is "*The Question*" we must answer before we leave this chapter. Who rules your life? Often we become captain and navigator of our own destinies and then blame God for every raging storm we encounter. Too often people have seated themselves on the throne of their lives and have simply rubber-stamped a cross over their image in order to justify calling it Christianity.

There is another phrase used often by believers: "I believe God is opening doors, and I need to follow." Is this the same feeling? Is it just another emotional response to something we've been inspired to recreate? Or instead, could it be God leading us the way we've asked Him to? I believe this is a very different force directing us, and learning to tell the difference isn't easy. We are not talking about a warped version of "self" that focuses on how great *I am*. We are talking about the one true God, *The Great I AM*. Too many times we just do what we want. We take the part of Christianity we like, 'the Grace', and then leave out the part we don't, 'the Holy'. This "Mr. Potato Head" approach to God leaves one confused and dazed because our expectations of life don't add up with the situations we find ourselves in.

Many see the Holy Spirit as a wild card that may color outside the lines of scripture. We need to remember that it was the Holy Spirit who wrote the Bible through inspired men, and the Spirit tells us that all scripture is inspired and will lead us in truth.

> But know this first of all, that no prophecy of Scripture is a matter of one's own interpretation, for no prophecy was ever made by an act of human will, but men moved by the Holy Spirit spoke from God.
> —II Peter 1:20–21

> All Scripture is inspired by God and profitable for teaching, for reproof, for correction, for training in righteousness; so that the man of God may be adequate, equipped for every good work.
> —II Timothy 3:16–17

I believe the Bible is the guide we must follow, and it teaches us that the Holy Spirit has been sent as a Comforter to guide us in truth. When we study the promise of the Holy Spirit's coming in

John chapter 16, we find that God the Spirit is not pushing His own agenda, but instead magnifies the teachings of Christ. When the Spirit pulls on our hearts or we believe God is leading us to action, that guidance must line up with the Spirit's greatest work, the Bible. It must coincide with the teachings of Christ.

Once we set our hearts and minds on the one true God, we can distinguish which "signs" are worth listening to on this road trip we call life. When we line up our lives with His will, some amazing things begin to happen. The highlights of life become sweeter, and though the pain still hurts, it doesn't sweep us away.

I hope to explain this amazing process of "God leading us" by revisiting scripture and the people we find there. I want to share some of my own experiences and try to give some helpful tips as well. Learning to *Seek and Find God* has provided some of the most exciting lessons I've ever experienced. Learning to *Be Still and Know God* has involved much tougher lessons that often last for years, yet they are more meaningful and rewarding. I know this chapter is a blunt start that some will refuse to accept; but how else can we start a study together on hearing God except by making sure we are talking about the same One? This book contains chapters of experiences and chapters that will be more scripture based. Now as we end the introduction, let me share my journey with you. Let's begin with a prayer that is very personal to me.

Prayer

My dear God and Father, thank You for allowing me the privilege to call You my Father. Thank You for caring enough to give me the avenue of prayer and wanting me to bring You my praise and problems. I have a decision to make, a choice that I can't take back and I dare not decide alone. I need Your wisdom and guidance, I give You control of my life, and I ask Your forgiveness when I've seated myself on Your throne. Lord, my prayer is simple. Please open some doors that can shed some light on where/what I need to do. Please shut doors and stop me from taking paths that are not in Your will. My dear Lord, sometimes I don't hear well and often miss seeing things too. So please speak loudly. Kick me through the door if needed, and when You shut one, make sure to hit my toes.

'Foundational'

But seek ye first the kingdom of God, and his righteousness; and all these things shall be added unto you.

—Matthew 6:33

You must come to see how wonderful you are in God and how helpless you are in yourself.

—Smith Wigglesworth

He who asks a question is a fool for five minutes; he who does not ask a question remains a fool forever.

—Chinese Proverb

Chapter 2

Seeking Answers

When Jesus Christ came and revealed to us the Father, He was met with a vast ocean of questions. For about four thousand years people had sat and wondered about the meaning of life and our purpose. For the first time ever God was in their midst and people were lining up to quiz Him. First, people questioned whether or not He was the Son of God. Then they questioned His teachings, His miracles, and His very character. The first question we find once Jesus began His ministry was asked by Nathaniel in John 1:46.

"Can anything good come out of Nazareth?" The reply to this question actually answers many questions that people bring to God today. "Come and see" (Ref 2:1). "Come and see" is just another way of saying, "Seek and find." Nathaniel sought an answer to his question, and afterward he gave up life as he knew it to follow Christ.

Ultimately we all will have some major questions for God. Some people discourage the thought of asking God anything. They would say, "It's not our place" or "Just have faith." I believe the Bible plainly teaches us to seek and find answers. Hebrews 11:1 teaches us that faith is the substance of things hoped for and the *evidence of things unseen*. Faith has a two-part definition. Often people cling only to the first part. To these individuals, faith is only something we hope for. They would argue that we cannot know anything for sure; we can only leap out there and pray we land on something. This mind-set would say, "If I know something, it's not faith," and therefore seeking answers would be a waste of time. This is not the faith scripture describes. Faith is also "evidence of things unseen." "Proof of things hidden" is another way to phrase it. Please note 1 John 5:13:

> These things I have written to you who believe in the name of the Son of God, so that you may know [not guess, or simply hope] that you have eternal life.

Consider the story of Peter walking on water.

> Immediately He made the disciples get into the boat and go ahead of Him to the other side, while He sent the crowds away. After He had sent the crowds away, He went up on the mountain by Himself to pray; and when it was evening, He was there alone. But the boat was already a long distance from the land, battered by the waves; for the wind was contrary. And in the fourth watch of the night He came to them, walking on the sea. When the disciples saw Him walking on the sea, they were terrified, and said, "It is a ghost!" And they cried out in fear. But immediately Jesus spoke to them, saying, "Take courage, it is I; do not be afraid."
>
> Peter said to Him, "Lord, if it is You, command me to come to You on the water." And He said, "Come!" And Peter got out of the boat, and walked on the water and came toward Jesus. But seeing the wind, he became frightened, and beginning to sink, he cried out, "Lord, save me!" Immediately Jesus stretched out His hand and took hold of him, and said to him, "You of little faith, why did you doubt?" When they got into the boat, the wind stopped. And those who were in the boat worshiped Him, saying, "You are certainly God's Son!"
> —Matthew 14:22–33

This illustration has been used maybe more than any other for "stepping out on faith." But did he step out blindly without a clue? Was it a leap in the dark, just hoping for the best? No, the evidence of God was standing on the water right in front of him, smiling in the midst of the storm.

Have you considered Peter's response to Christ? "Lord, if it is You, *command me* to come to You on the water"(emphasis mine). Awkward choice of words, you may think, unless you are Peter. As you consider what Peter saw from day to day, you begin to understand his thought process. Jesus speaks, and the blind see. Jesus speaks, and the deaf hear. Jesus speaks, and diseases flee. Jesus speaks, and nature itself bends to His will. Looking at the "evidence," Peter wanted to hear the command. He knew if Jesus commands it, then it must happen.

Just as Peter had proof standing before him, so do we. There are evidence and proofs all around us that God is alive and well. He didn't expect people to just blindly follow; He gave us a light. He gave us his Word.

> **Your word is a lamp to my feet and a light to my path.**
> **—Psalm 119:105**

Then He tells us to pursue Him.

> **Ask, and it will be given to you; seek, and you will find; knock, and it will be opened to you. For everyone who asks receives, and he who seeks finds, and to him who knocks it will be opened.**
> **Matthew 7:7–8**

This chapter will deal with asking our questions and learning how to listen and look for the answers that God gives. Questions should not be used as excuses to walk away from Jesus and Christianity. Instead they need to be asked, answered, and then allowed to change our lives. The real question is, Will we seek and find those answers? But first let's look at how to ask them.

Let's look at two questions and consider the differences.

> **What do you say about Him, since He opened your eyes?** [Pharisees' question to the blind man]
>
> —John 9:17

> **Who are you, Lord?** [Saul's question]
>
> —Acts 9:5

First, consider these two questions side by side. Are they not the same question? The heart of both inquiries is the same. Who is this Jesus character? Both are asked by a Pharisee. They have the same background and theology. However, are they both sincere in the search? Do they really want to know? One thing I want to point out is that the Pharisees didn't even have the courage to bring Jesus the question again, so instead they asked the man born blind.

The Jews had a preconceived notion that the Christ was coming to establish an earthly kingdom. They assumed God would come in the same fashion He always came, freeing them from their oppressor. They expected a "Deliverer" like Moses, who led the people out of bondage. And as they moved forward, God destroyed the Egyptians behind them. They longed for another king like David, who drove out the Philistines, or a King Solomon, whose name was known throughout the earth. As the Assyrians were destroyed and Babylon torn was down, they now hoped to see Rome suffer. When Jesus came, they began to ask Him their questions to see if He measured up to their expectations. They found themselves doubting because, frankly, this wasn't the Jesus they were looking for. As we look closely at this question, we realize the Pharisees were not looking for an answer; they were looking for *their* answer.

When we ask the question "Who are you, God?" we often already have an answer that we are expecting. And if we don't get the answer we are looking for, then God must not exist.

Why do bad things happen to good people?

We have already decided that if it's me suffering, nothing bad should happen.

Why isn't the world full of peace?

We have already decided that God came to this world to bring us an earthly peace.

Why can't you give me a sign, God, so I'll know You are there, and You are all You claim to be?

We have already decided if God can't jump through some hoops for me, why should I for Him?

There is no problem with asking God questions. There is a problem, however, when we ask and have already answered for Him. We can't produce both sides of the conversation. If we let Him respond, we find answers—maybe not the ones we wanted, but when has humanity ever desired what is best for itself?

The second difference between these two questions can be observed by considering the intent of the Pharisees' hearts. Do you remember whom they ask? Why would they take their questions to the man born blind instead of to Jesus? They quiz him for hours, it appears. Guilt and frustration often make us ashamed or too angry to go directly to the person we have an issue with. And let's be honest—how well does a frustrated or angry person listen? We have all been there. The entire time I should be opening my ears, I am instead rehearsing my accusations in my own mind. Instead of considering their words, I am waiting for the opening to blast them.

They wanted an excuse and only got angry with God when their excuses failed. Some ask the question "If God can do anything, can He make a squared circle?" I've learned over the years that people who ask these questions don't want an answer. Their question is a trophy held high so all can observe their brilliance. Answering their question only frustrates them. Take a small food can that is as wide as it is tall. Now rotate it observing it from all angles. We can make a squared circle. From the side angle it's square, and by looking straight down on the can's diameter, we find a circle. The person hates this answer. "That's not what I mean." What do they mean? They struggle to find the right wording to define the impossible in their opinion. How then is God supposed to give them an answer when they can't even ask the question? Consider what God has done. Forget a squared circle; God has broken down the walls of sin that imprisoned and separated us from Himself. Combining two shapes? Try Jesus Christ, a man … who was God. The world still can't grasp that either.

If we don't allow God to answer in His own way, and accept that answer, we allow bitterness to consume us, pull us away from Him, and ultimately destroy us.

A Fictional Story

A woman with two small children wakes up early one morning. She finds herself in tears when there is no food to give to her children when they awaken. Desperately she begins to pray near the old chimney that God will send her food.

Two teenagers passing by hear the woman praying. They laugh at the scene of a woman praying for God to send food down a chimney. So they run home and bag up some food to play a joke on their newfound victim. They return and find the woman still praying as the children are waking up. They climb up onto the roof and drop the bag of groceries down the chimney holding back their urge to burst into laughter. They hear the woman begin praising God for the food and finally yell condescendingly down to her, "You foolish woman, do you really think God sends food in paper bags down chimneys? God didn't send that food to you, we did." As they finish their assault of jeers and mockery, they listen for the woman's response. They notice the woman is laughing as she responds to God, "Isn't that just like you, Lord, sending us food in paper bags down the chimney and using the devil as your delivery service" -(Ref. 2:2).

This woman had a choice. First, she could accept God's answer and give Him praise. Second, she could accept the boys' reasoning and become bitter, as the thought of looking foolish destroyed her faith.

So many times the answers are clearer when we are broken. Saul's question is asked in brokenness. Take a moment to look at his story found in Acts.

> Saul was still breathing out murderous threats against the Lord's disciples. He went to the high priest and asked him for letters to the synagogues in Damascus, so that if he found any there who belong to the Way, whether men or women, he might take them as prisoners to Jerusalem. As he neared Damascus on his journey, suddenly a light from heaven flashed around him. He fell to the ground and heard a voice say to him, "Saul, Saul, why do you persecute me?" "Who are you, Lord?" Saul asked.
>
> —Acts 9:1-5

Humbled. Broken. We wonder why God permits us to suffer; sometimes it's to open our ears. What is the difference when Saul asked, "Who are you, Lord?" His background in theology was the same. He too was a Pharisee looking for an earthly kingdom. The difference is God humbled him enough to get his pride out of the way for a moment and consider the fact that he was wrong.

As we conclude our thoughts from John 9 and Acts 9, we need to understand the lesson on our topic at hand. How do we better hear what our Lord is saying? Watch as Jesus concluded the lesson for the Pharisees.

> Jesus said, "For judgment I have come into this world, so that the blind will see and those who see will become

> blind." Some Pharisees who were with Him heard Him
> say this and asked, "What? Are we blind too?" Jesus
> said, "If you were blind, you would not be guilty of
> sin; but now that you claim you can see, your guilt
> remains."
>
> —John 9:39–40

The Pharisees were totally blind when it came to hearing the
words of Jesus, yet they didn't realize it. For this reason they never
asked for sight. We, like the Pharisees, have to stop listening with
our eyes; cease trying to translate God's words through our pride.
If we don't, our pride could blind us. Look back on the story of the
Pharisees in John 9 and consider their words in verse 24.

> So they called a second time the man that was born
> blind, and said to him, "Give glory to God: *we know
> that* this man is a sinner." (emphasis mine)

They had heard the answer once already, but it didn't make
sense to them. Why? Because they just knew Jesus was a sinner.
Think about that for a moment. No one could even find fault with
Him the night before the crucifixion. No one could trap him in
speech or trick questions. No one had any legitimate accusation to
bring against Him of anything, and yet they made the statement
"We know Jesus is a sinner." Why would they say this? They said it
because human pride has always rejected God's will when it comes
to things we don't understand. And to justify our rejection of His
will we blame Him because "He must be wrong". Pride alters the
message and blinds us to God's will. You will never hear God clearly
until you rid yourself of this distraction.

Now let's look at the conclusion of Saul's story.

> Saul got up from the ground, but when he opened his
> eyes he could see nothing. So they led him by the hand

into Damascus. **For three days he was blind, and did
not eat or drink anything.**

—Acts 9:8, 9

God actually took away Saul's sight to help Him see. When
Saul was blinded, sitting in the corner of that house for three days,
what went through his mind? With nowhere to look but inward,
Saul examined his own life. Instead of warring against Christians,
he stopped for a moment and realized he was warring against the
God of heaven. In other words, God humbled him and took pride
out of the way so he could hear. After looking at his own deeds and
sin, Saul repented. He was ready to receive God, even if God wasn't
what he had envisioned. "No more excuses, God, help me see You
and Your will, despite my desires." The answers that Saul found were
life-changing. God was and is more than he had ever envisioned.

One of the biggest steps in setting aside our pride is opening up
ourselves in a vulnerable way. As we open up in prayer to God, we
are doing exactly that. So please consider these chapter prayers. If
you are like me, you would rather use your own words. No problem,
but read them just the same. I hope they can inspire an attitude that
you can lead into your prayer with. Once you are there, take your
time :) The next chapter can wait.

Prayer

*Lord, please help me see just You, hear just You. In this moment of
prayer help me stop putting the words I long for on Your lips and
instead calm my anxious heart. As this week/month/year rolls on,
help me adopt a childlike wonder and curiosity. And as I let You
unfold Your plan, allow me to rest in Your hands while You work.*

'Foundational'

What good thing must I do to inherit life eternal?
—Rich Young Ruler

What must we do?
—Jews on Pentecost

Look inside yourself; you are more than what you have become!
—Mufasa (Lion King)

Chapter 3

What Do You Want from Me?

It's a question that I believe everyone will ask God at least once in this life. Many will ask the question repeatedly; but don't think we are all asking the same question. Our reasons vary. Consider our two introduction verses again. The rich young ruler's story is found in Matthew.

> And someone came to Him and said, "Teacher, what good thing shall I do that I may obtain eternal life?" And He said to him, "Why are you asking Me about what is good? There is only One who is good; but if you wish to enter into life, keep the commandments." Then he said to Him, "Which ones?" And Jesus said, "YOU SHALL NOT COMMIT MURDER; YOU SHALL NOT COMMIT ADULTERY; YOU SHALL NOT STEAL; YOU SHALL NOT BEAR FALSE WITNESS; HONOR YOUR FATHER AND MOTHER; and YOU SHALL LOVE YOUR NEIGHBOR AS YOURSELF." The young man said to Him, "All these things I have kept; what am I still lacking?" Jesus said to him, "If you wish to be complete, go and sell your possessions and give to the poor, and you will have treasure in heaven; and come, follow Me." But when the young man heard this

statement, he went away grieving; for he was one who owned much property.

—Matthew 19:16–22

Our second verse is found in the book of Acts after Peter hits them with some hard truths as he preaches on Pentecost.

Now when they heard this, they were pierced to the heart, and said to Peter and the rest of the apostles, "Brethren, what shall we do?"

—Acts 2:37

Often people ask the right question, but for the wrong reason. Sometimes, like the rich young ruler, we boast of our accomplishments: *"What other good deeds would you like me to perform?"* Sometimes in anger or frustration we blast the question in a self-righteous defense: *"What else could you possibly want from me!?"* Other times we cry out in shame or desperation, humbled only by our downfalls: *"What must I do?"* And on rare occasions we get it right, whispering it in privacy, broken and in awe of His majesty: *"What else could I give, that You would want?"* It is a question we need to ask, but to do so we have to step out of our world and consider the Creator's point of view.

Conflict management counselors will tell you that 99 percent of the time conflict arises because one or more parties don't have all the facts. Once both sides of the party are on the same page, a solution soon follows. Often we find ourselves baffled at the cards we've been dealt by God and we begin to ask the question "Lord, what do You want from me?" And we think how much easier life would be if He would just give us a better hand, or at least tell us what cards are coming. Do I go all in, God, and leave this job, or do I wait? Before we finish this question, let's back up and consider the dealer's point of view.

The Gospel of Luke tells about the parable of the wedding feast. Let's look at it again for a moment.

> But He said to him, "A man was giving a big dinner, and he invited many; and at the dinner hour he sent his slave to say to those who had been invited, 'Come; for everything is ready now.' But they all alike began to make excuses. The first one said to him, 'I have bought a piece of land and I need to go out and look at it; please consider me excused.' Another one said, 'I have bought five yoke of oxen, and I am going to try them out; please consider me excused.' Another one said, 'I have married a wife, and for that reason I cannot come.' And the slave came back and reported this to his master. Then the head of the household became angry and said to his slave, 'Go out at once into the streets and lanes of the city and bring in here the poor and crippled and blind and lame.' And the slave said, 'Master, what you commanded has been done, and still there is room.' And the master said to the slave, 'Go out into the highways and along the hedges, and compel them to come in, so that my house may be filled. For I tell you, none of those men who were invited shall taste of my dinner.'"
>
> —Luke 14:16–24

Now, I have to admit this passage often bothered me earlier in my studies, and I really didn't spend much time teaching on it. I could sympathize with these people, especially the newlywed couple. These people had been invited to a banquet, but sometimes our lives are just too busy. Other important events are taking place, like my honeymoon. It just seemed harsh … in my little world.

Now, most of you have heard the textbook definition of a parable—an earthly story with a heavenly meaning. I want to apply that principle here and look over this passage again, but through

God's eyes. First, the man holding a great feast must be God. I think we all agree on this, and that would make the wedding feast His kingdom. God is inviting us into His kingdom, His church, the very body of Christ. Second, we have those who were invited. These people are sometimes referred to as the early Jews who rejected Christ. And though that makes sense, I want us to consider putting ourselves in this story instead. Parables are rich and can be applied in many ways.

Consider the "chosen" who have been invited to attend the feast. They respond in the form of three excuses: "I have new property," "I've invested in new equipment," and "I have personal things going on within my family."

The question we need to ask to understand God's point of view is, "Who gave these people their gifts?" Who blessed them with property, goods, and a wife/family? These are all gifts from God ... the same God who has now invited them to His great feast.

How do you suppose God feels when the replies come in: "*So sorry, God; I won't be attending Your feast because You have blessed me with a new house and I really need to fix some things on the second floor.*" Or, "*Lord, I am swamped with paperwork from the new job. You know, the one I've prayed You would give me for the last year. Anyway, I am afraid I won't make Your feast.*" And finally, "*Father, thank You for my wife and children; they are such a blessing. But the energy it takes to get everyone out the door and to Your feast is just beyond my capabilities right now.*" Does God have the right to be angry when we use His blessings as an excuse to ignore Him? Well when you put it that way ... absolutely!

Now let's take it a step further. Imagine God's thought process when this prayer reaches His ears: "*God, thank You for the job You've given me. And the small raise I got this year has been a big help. I know I've not attended church like I should and the kids really need to get involved, but things are so stressful at home. Could You help me get a promotion? There's an opening coming up, and that pay increase would really lighten the load on our family. Thank You, Lord. Amen.*"

It seems like a humble prayer and heartfelt. But I can't help but feel God's pain when He hears, "Thank You for my blessings … (that I've used as an excuse to skip out on You) … and by the way could You bless me more?" Do you think it's in our best interest for God to give us more blessings, when clearly blessings have become our stumbling block?

Every blessing from God comes with a price tag. You want a job? You must give up time and energy. A family means sacrificing a lot of independence and freedom. Even simple blessings like a car mean maintenance. How foolish people are when they think winning the lottery would simplify life. And then after all the trials and price tags that blessing brings you in this life, you then answer or give an account for how you used all those blessings in judgment.

I am reminded of a scene from my childhood at a gas station off I-24 heading into Chattanooga, Tennessee. The interstate dips down into Georgia for a moment, and many people stopped for cheaper gas prices back then. Georgia also had a state lottery, whereas Tennessee did not. I remember walking into the gas station with my mother and noticing a man walking out. My first impression of him was that he might have been homeless. His clothes definitely reflected that money was an issue. He was dressed in layers of ragged clothing for warmth, and in his hands he held some lottery tickets. I doubt I would have ever remembered this man if I had not passed by him again as we left. Heading back to our vehicle, I saw him shutting the door of a run-down old car and tossing the tickets in the trash as he reentered the store, a look of desperation on his face. Hopelessness is an expression that hits you in the soul when observed. As I passed the car, I noticed the same look on a woman's face in the front seat. I heard two children sitting in the back, trying to get her attention, and just as they were falling out of my peripheral vision, I heard the girl telling her mother that she was hungry and wanted something to eat.

Many of us need to consider our lives and our requests to God as we ask these questions: *"Why don't You help me?" "Do You care?"*

"Are You listening?" and *"What do You want from me?"* It seems we want to accept only answers that financially bless us, and that the life we currently have must be a mistake, because we consider ourselves good people who do not deserve hard times.

Listen to the question again: *"What do you want from me?"* asks the man from whom God has taken away all the blessings, aka stumbling blocks. He may be asking to find pity, not answers. He may just want to make God feel guilty for putting him in this situation. He may not be asking at all, just blowing off steam because he feels hopeless. The rich young ruler asked the question just so Christ would notice how well he was doing. I can only imagine the deafening ring in God's ears from hearing this question over and over; yet no one wants an answer, because no one is really asking the question.

In Acts 2:37, the Jews finally asked the question on the day of Pentecost: "Brother, what do we need to do?!" The question is addressed to Peter and the other apostles. There is no hidden agenda; the inquiry is pure. It is broken, stripped down to nothing. Naked and vulnerable, they actually want to know. I believe this process hurts God more than we know. All parents are presented a similar experience with their own children. Maybe God designed it this way so we can better understand Him in these moments. Many times children will not listen to their parents concerning everything from extreme issues like sex and substance abuse, to even simple matters like sitting at home playing video games and demanding money to go play on the weekends. In the process of breaking, they turn the finger to the parent who warned them. They blame the adults for not providing a way to continue their self-indulgent desires. And in humility, once the *breaking* process is complete, they finally open their ears—not to our voice as much as to their own demise.

We can't bring our questions to God with only our point of view in mind. This corrupts our hearing, and with only our preconceived notions to go on, we stand before God demanding answers with our fingers in our ears. This is the dealer's point of view I mentioned earlier. This is where the all-knowing Father, the Alpha and the Omega sits and listens to the questions we bring Him. When we start considering God's will over our own, we have at least entered the right mind-set to listen as God begins to answer the question "Should I push forward or be still?"

Some of you are already at this point, and I hope the rest of this book is uplifting and enlightening. Some of you are giving a lot of thought to this chapter. You may even be trying to decide if you agree with it or not. I hope this challenges the way you think, but not in a discouraging way. I hope you give this chapter a day to sink in and pray about it. The real struggles are still coming, because sometimes the broken still don't hear answers and the situations have nothing to do with financial or physical blessings. I reserved my all-time favorite prayer/poem for this chapter, and I hope you will examine it closely. I wrote it early in my ministry and find it to be closer to my heart each year. It has a puzzle element to it that may drive an English teacher crazy. If so, just keep reading it until you find there really aren't any errors at all.

My Prayer

> lord, bring Me to My knees, because there
> is no securer place than within your presence.
> take away '*My Pride*' from underneath me. As
> You break my heart from within, move me …
> to my knees … for joy, for shame, and for awe.
> Lord, take my strength to stand
> and catch me when i fall.
>
> —byron smith

'Seek and Find'

Can you fathom the mysteries of God? Can you probe the limits of the Almighty?
—Job 11:7

Hardships often prepare ordinary people for an extraordinary destiny.
—C. S. Lewis

Do or do not. There is no try.
—Yoda

Chapter 4

What's Stopping You?

The first three chapters of this book are focused on adjusting our mind-set to hear God in our lives. As we move into the fourth chapter, we will start looking at the "Seek and Find" lessons that God has in store for us. Please understand that these lessons could be taught by God at any time. God may have to come back later in our lives and give us a follow-up lesson. The layout of this book simply reflects the order in which most people learn them.

It seems like the first few lessons God has in store for each of us revolve around the thought of seek and find. As I look through story after story in scripture, it's the same. The beginning of our walk with Him takes action on our part. Matthew gives us a timeless verse:

> **Ask, and it will be given you; seek, and you will find; knock, and the door will be opened for you**
>
> **—Matthew 7:7**

Moses heard the call through a burning bush, but he had to seek answers by going back to Egypt. This story is the perfect example for people asking the question "What does God want from me?" I believe God has put into each heart a passion. Now, don't go crazy with just this idea. We have a lot of passions, but just following what we want to do and blaming the outcome on God's design of the human heart isn't right. Moses had a deep love for his people, Israel. This passion drove him to kill an Egyptian and flee Egypt. This is a good example of the wrong way to follow your heart. What he wanted next was to disappear, forget, and find a new life. When God called Moses, He called him to do a job that Moses wouldn't have dared dream about, much less do. It wasn't going to be pleasant or comfortable. But please realize that God did give Moses a mission that lined up with his passion for Israel. When we hear that call or feel that push, we need to go find answers.

We find the greatest question within us begging to be resolved, and often we are afraid to ask it. Is God there? And if so, is God all He claims to be? *Seek and find.*

The year was 1995. I just graduated from high school and was preparing to start college. It was early August, and I was at a small college in Tennessee trying to fill out my paperwork. This wasn't the plan. This wasn't where I wanted to be at all. I was heartbroken as my dreams shattered around me, and I felt abandoned by God. Of course who could blame Him; I hadn't been living the Christian life for months now. So there I was, in a spiritual slump, on a roller coaster of emotions wondering if God was there.

Let me explain. School had never been easy for me. We were poor, living in a trailer on a farm owned by some members of the church we attended. Social awkwardness is something every student faces, but add to that a very short, very poor Christian-minded teenage boy trying fit in. I believe I was liked by all but loved by none. I was the class favorite, yet I never made it to many social gatherings. My classmates respected me and appreciated my presence around the school, but I never really felt I belonged anywhere.

Over the past two years I had been looking forward to attending Faulkner University in Montgomery, Alabama. I had struggled with what I was going to do with my life, what career I would pursue. I had been working as a farmhand since I was fourteen on and off. I had also worked as a short-order cook, a waiter at Shoney's, and a carpenter in the summer months with my father. My parents had divorced when I was seven, so up until my junior year I hadn't spent a lot of time with my dad at all.

Just before my junior year I had attended a summer Bible camp. Camp Wetoga had been a sanctuary for me over the years, since age seven. It was the only place I knew I belonged, and I would have lived there if they had let me. Each year I'd meet college students from Faulkner University. They would talk about the Christian college and give out small scholarships to campers. That summer they gave it to me. I felt that God may have been opening a door, and so after a few months of thought I decided this was the path I wanted to take. I set my goals on pursuing a career in ministry. Things continued to fall into place, and I even picked up more scholarships through other camp weeks as time moved on.

As I began turning the corner of my senior year, I realized how little the scholarship money was compared to the actual cost of a private college. Nevertheless, I was going to Faulkner and everything was going to be great. Faulkner had become my answer to a lot of problems. It was a place where I could forget everything and start a new life. I had to begin working full time as soon as summer began because I was short about five thousand dollars.

Now, for the most part of my senior year I had fallen into an immoral life. I had been seeing a girl for the better part of my senior year, and the relationship had become a sexual one. It was my advances that were to blame. Here I was trying to show her the God I claimed to love while pursuing her in an ungodly way. I felt like I was watching life from a theater in the back of my mind, a hypocrite that seemed pitied instead of judged by friends. I was clinging to two separate worlds that couldn't coexist. As the summer ended, I found myself at the crossroads of my life.

I had worked all summer, but because of car problems and some family expenses, I had saved nothing. After applying for everything I knew to apply for, five thousand dollars still stood in my way. The Faulkner dream was slipping away as I realized there was no way I could find the money. The day I was supposed to be registering at Faulkner, I was registering at Chattanooga State. As I filled out the admission papers, my heart was breaking. I had visited this Christian college and had fallen in love with it, and yet I stood on another campus that reminded me of high school all over again. As I sat there angry and bitter, I questioned God. I challenged my faith. I even doubted whether there was a God. And then it happened ...

Like a small still voice in my head, the whisper began,

What's stopping you?

To begin with, the voice seemed more like a cruel taunt. Five thousand dollars is stopping me, for starters. *Is that all? Is God not bigger than that?*

Of course God is bigger than that, but... My mind went blank. How could I answer that?

What's stopping you?

God isn't with me. I know the life I've been living, and I know it hasn't pleased Him.

So wouldn't God want you to go and draw closer to Him?

I hate it when answers come back so fast you feel dumb for even asking the question. At the same time, those answers are even more convicting. I know that God couldn't have a problem with me going to a university where I was going to draw closer to Him and give Him the rest of my life in ministering to His people.

What's stopping you?

Well, frankly, I don't see how this is even possible ...

Come and see.

At this point my heart was pounding with nervous excitement. Was this His voice, or was it stupidity? Suddenly all that mattered was answering this question. I knew this moment would affect the rest of my life. I could follow this path and find God bigger and more amazing than I'd ever realized, or I could follow and find that God isn't trying to lead my life at all and that perhaps I'm a fool for believing in Him. My mind drifted back to Peter being beckoned by Christ to step out onto a raging sea. Did I dare step out of the boat in the midst of this storm?

Why are you still here?

I threw my registration papers in the trash and headed to my dad's. I packed up everything I owned and called my dad at work. I told him I was headed to Faulkner. He inquired how, and I told him the truth. I had no idea. I might be back the following day. He seemed to understand in a small way and told me to be careful. I called my mother and got a different reaction. I'm sure you could imagine a mother's response to her eighteen-year-old son leaving registration at a local college and heading 240 miles away with nothing but a prayer, but I didn't care. I was on a collision course with God, and I wanted to see if there was, in fact, a collision.

The trip from Chattanooga to Montgomery took almost four hours. That was a lot of time to review my life and ponder the path I'd chosen. I got there later in the afternoon and found my dorm room. I had preregistered months before, so I was expected. The problem was a lot of money that stood between me and starting classes. That night I unpacked, and after talking to a couple of guys I had met through camps I went to bed.

As I was lying there, I heard a knock at the door. Jonathan Walden entered and sat down to talk. I had met Jonathan on a previous trip to Faulkner. He was a student there and only two years ahead of me. I had spent a little time with him and shared a little bit of my story. He was a very kindhearted individual who had been given the nickname of "mother" by guys in his fraternity. Jonathan asked if I was comfortable and settled in. I jokingly said, "Yeah, until tomorrow when they ask for their money."

Jonathan smiled and replied, "I wouldn't worry about that. You see, there's a man named Jimmy Faulkner, who heard about your situation. He is paying the five thousand dollars that you needed." Then Jonathan finished by saying that it wasn't just a one-time deal. Every year that I went to Faulkner, this guy was going to pay what I couldn't. As long as I did everything I could to find funds, he would pick up the tab. Jonathan left and I wept. This was the turning point of my life. It would be just over a decade later when I would finally meet and thank Mr. Faulkner for allowing God to use him in my life.

What's stopping you?

Come and see?

Seek and find?

Voices, questions, and challenges come from God as He leads me. So how do you know? How can you tell the difference between just following what your heart feels or knowing God is the one calling you down a path?

First, let me say God has a personal path or direction designed for each individual. Remember we serve a very creative God. Don't think I'm telling all of my readers to run to a Christian college and they'll get all the help they need to finish school. Your path will be different, designed just for you. However, there are some things you should listen for or look for that always seem to emphasize the fact that God is directing your path.

For instance, when God is leading us, the path usually isn't laid out clearly before us. As a matter of fact, oftentimes the path looks impossible. It's the Red Sea before Moses, the walls of Jericho before Joshua, the promise of a son to Abraham, or a Goliath standing in front of a young David. God points the way, and we want to turn and look at Him like He's crazy. *Are You sure? Am I sure that You're sure? This can't be right!*

Following God's lead is a lot different than just following your heart. Following your heart often takes you down a path that makes sense to you, and you can see how the whole thing is going to fall together perfectly. This is what you want; it's you grabbing life by the horns and making your mark. Let's use Moses again and compare these paths.

First, we have Moses leading his own life. Moses has a passion for Israel. Consider what he feels as he strikes out at the Egyptian, killing him and saving his kinsmen from persecution. Consider these additional verses:

> By faith Moses, when he had grown up, refused to be called the son of Pharaoh's daughter, choosing rather to endure ill-treatment with the people of God than to enjoy the passing pleasures of sin, considering the reproach of Christ greater riches than the treasures of Egypt; for he was looking to the reward. By faith he left Egypt, not fearing the wrath of the king; for he endured, as seeing Him who is unseen.
>
> —Hebrews 11:24–27

Please notice all the things Moses did in faith. They imply he acted out of belief in these areas. The slaying of the Egyptian isn't listed here, but others are. His beliefs played a large role in the choices he made. He felt all the emotions of pity, guilt, and rage, and yet excitement at the point where he finally stood up for what he believed. What the Egyptian was doing wasn't right, so he intervened. Moses knew there would be consequences, and so he followed his gut feeling again and left Egypt. Maybe he saw this self-inflicted exile as a sacrifice he made to do God's will. Now he could tell himself that this was simply the price he had to pay in order to do what was right. Carrying an unseen load for a higher purpose gave him a sense of righteousness, and seeing that a higher power had given him a new home, peace, and a wife was like a divine stamp of approval.

Now compare that small feat to the plan God actually designed. First, all those emotions of pity, guilt, and rage might have been present, but they were masked by an overwhelming sense of God's presence. When we are led by the Spirit, our attention is on Him, not on justice or rage. If I have the whole plan put together, then I am following exactly that, my own plan. Second, the path wasn't something that I could accomplish alone. When asked later, "Who delivered the Israelite years ago when you killed the Egyptian and buried him in the sand?" Moses would have to respond, "I did." Then ask Moses, "Who delivered the nation of Israel and buried the Egyptian army in the sea?" Moses would answer, "God did." I'm not saying that our plans and God's plans don't overlap at times. They will, because God's plans aren't derailed so easily, **"and we know that God causes all things to work together for good to those who love God, to those who are called according to His purpose. "(Romans 8:28).** Yet we must understand the difference is that the road we take to get there will be God's and not our own.

Another difference is how things continued to come together. Please don't think I have placed all my hopes in God in the solo act of a man who helped me get through college. The lessons have gotten more profound over the years, and the barriers before me have grown much larger than thousands of dollars to get through college. As I look back on college now, I see this difference. Let's say I had been able to make the money to attend Faulkner. Would the road have been the same? Of course not, but we have to get through this chapter before we start that lesson.

As we conclude these thoughts, please consider this. Many times we see an easier road and wonder why God doesn't put us on it. If He would simply grant more money, I could spend less time trying to make ends meet and more time blessing His church, people, and kingdom. But perhaps God isn't worried so much with what I could do for His kingdom. Maybe He is more focused on who I am becoming in the journey. The extreme example could be made from the scenario "Lord, if you would let me win a million dollars, I'll give half back." Why does God need you to give half a million dollars? Because you see hurt and pain in the world? Aren't those the things that humble us and bring us close to Him? And the better question to consider is "What would the other half million do to me?"

This prayer is for someone who is ready to move and yet willing to let go at the same time. If God is ready for us to move and we are in the 'Seek and Find' chapters of God's plan, we have to begin praying like this.

Prayer

Dear Father, give me the insight to see when I am pushing my own agenda and the self-restraint to stop. Help me to not lean on my own understanding more than I depend on Your words. Lord, I'm not asking for destinations or explanations; I'm just asking You to reveal the direction I need to move (if I do in fact need to move). And when You have opened the door, give me the courage to go forward.

Seek and Find

The Lord said to Gideon, "The troops with you are too many for me to give the Midianites into their hand, Israel would only take the credit away from me, saying 'My own hand has delivered me'"

—Judges 7:2

God's ability is not limited by man's ability to understand.
—Unknown

Not yet, wait for the opportune moment.
—Jack Sparrow

Chapter 5

Here ... You Try

The Gospel of John contains one of my favorite stories. After finishing the previous chapter you will soon see why.

> When He looked up and saw a large crowd coming toward Him, Jesus said to Philip, "Where are we to buy bread for these people to eat?" He said this to test him, for he himself knew what he was going to do. Philip answered Him, "Six months' wages would not buy enough bread for each of them to get a little." One of His disciples, Andrew, Simon Peter's brother, said to Him, "There is a boy here who has five barley loaves and two fish. But what are they among so many people?"
>
> —John 6:5–9

Okay, let's slow it down for a moment and review. Jesus has presented a question/challenge to the apostles, namely Philip. "How do we feed these people?" As we reference this story from other Gospel accounts, we find that the crowd is numbered at five thousand men plus women and children.

I can imagine a large mall where everyone is making their way to the food court, yet there's no food. Jesus asks Philip to feed them. Can you imagine what goes through Philip's mind? *He must be kidding, just joking with me.* Philip is waiting for the corners of Jesus's lips to smile and give Him away. *It would be nice if He would just smile. That would lead to a sigh of relief and move the spotlight somewhere else besides me. He's still not smiling.* Like a student in a classroom caught off guard by the teacher's question, Philip glances at the other apostles for help. Finally, he just states the obvious. "Even if I had six months' wages, I couldn't afford this." In short, "I don't have the money."

Jesus gives no response. I see Him just waiting there looking at Philip with a very confident disposition. You know the look—that look of an encouraging teacher, one you respect. There is a correct answer, and it's very apparent that Jesus has it. But He's waiting for the class to catch up. His eyes fixed on Philip pleading, *You know this!* The apostles see this, and they start searching for hints (Ref. 5:1).

I know how they felt. I described it in my own life just a moment ago. They were where Moses stood, the Egyptian army behind him and God pointing him toward the path he needed to take. The only problem was, God was pointing at the Red Sea, about twelve hundred miles in length and an estimated ten miles wide where they crossed (Ref. 5:2). At first, you are waiting for God to smile and say, "Just kidding." But instead you find Him simply challenging everything you're sure of. Everything you know, everything that makes sense says, "There's no path in this direction, Lord. It's a dead end; it's impossible."

That was where the apostles ended up as well. Philip stated that they didn't have the money. Andrew said there were a few fish and loaves here, but that was just a kid's lunch. The apostles simply threw up their hands as I did and concluded, "Well, frankly, Lord, I don't see how this is even possible."

I believe God does this on purpose, and the process makes me smile. Oftentimes God wants us to understand the process more than just see the outcome. He wants us to know that He was behind it. Being led by the Spirit isn't a fluke or something that can be credited to coincidence. So many times we fall in that trap. *"God, please help me in this financial crunch!"* And God answers. We get a job or a raise, and then in response we say, *"It's about time they took notice of my talents."* We ask again, *"God, please help my loved one as they go through surgery."* They come out fine, and we thank the doctor and staff for their skills and attentiveness. But on the occasions when someone dies, we give God all the credit. We blame Him blindly out of anger and walk away.

I believe *sometimes* God has to put a problem before us that is impossible. Then He gives us a chance to find a solution and He waits. This is important. Moses had to realize there was no place to go. The apostles had to understand that there was no solution within their own reach, and I had to understand that it was God who led me to college, and into ministry.

If He hadn't, I wouldn't have credited Him at all, and in the long run I would be leading my own life. Remember how I worked all summer before college began in the fall. I wasn't able to save any money. Unforeseen events stopped me. Why? If I had been able to save the money and then go on to Faulkner, would it have changed things? Absolutely! I can hear myself now: *"I worked my own way through college, pulled myself up by my own bootstraps,"* as the older generation puts it. I may have told others, *"Working my own way through college helped make me the man I am today."* I did work, you know. I spent mornings and evenings at the YMCA. I had a job on campus as well some years. I can hear the pride of self-accomplishment in my statements, and they would have become a stumbling block before me. Please don't misunderstand me, because there are people who have put themselves through college. I'm not speaking poorly of them or taking away credit where their credit is due. I'm simply saying the road God had me on was "custom-designed," and for this first big lesson in my life, He chose a college campus as His classroom. God put me through college. I worked and raised money, but I always understood from day one it was God.

It's Gideon's story as God reduced his army. Thirty-two thousand men were too many for God's glory to be seen.

> The Lord said to Gideon, "The troops with you are too many for me to give the Midianites into their hand, Israel would only take the credit away from me, saying 'My own hand has delivered me.'"
>
> —Judges 7:2

God reduced the army to ten thousand. Still God said there were too many. How would the people know God was leading them or if it was Gideon? The Lord reduced the army again to three hundred men. Reading on into the story reveals the size of their enemy.

> Now the Midianites and the Amalekites and all the sons of the east were lying in the valley as numerous as locusts; and their camels were without number, as numerous as the sand on the seashore.
>
> —Judges 7:12

This amazing force was crushed by God! Notice I said, "by God," and not by three hundred men. You see, at this point there is no denying God the victory.

So many times I believe we just avoid hardships or we hide in hobbies or even addictions when life gets tough. We don't like problems that aren't easily solved, because we live in a culture of instant gratification'. Imagine Gideon with the mind-set of today's average American.

God: Gideon, go destroy the enemy nation of Midian.

God allows Gideon and his army to march two hours and let the upcoming battle sink in.

Gideon: Lord, I've been thinking and You're right. We have thirty-two thousand able men ready to follow you. I know the enemy outnumbers us at least twenty to one, but I believe we can pull this off, with a lot of heart and dedication.

God: So you think "we" can do this? … Gideon, I've decided your forces are too great; we need to cut down the size of your army to ten thousand. Tell the rest to go home, because I don't need this many.

God allows another hour to pass so Gideon can process this new information. Gideon's mind is perplexed as he runs the numbers and considers new strategies.

Gideon: Lord, are you serious?! We were already vastly outnumbered, and by cutting the army to ten thousand we would each have to kill an average of sixty-four enemy soldiers. I've examined this army, and I know that they are not capable of this … Well, most aren't. I think a handful of these guys, myself included, could take on our portions … and if—

God: Gideon, your army is still too big to accomplish the agenda I have in mind. Divide them again.

Gideon:(crickets chirping)

God: Those three hundred will do. This is your army.

Gideon only needs about two minutes to brew before he responds.

Gideon: This isn't an army, God. This is just big enough to make a good marching band. I didn't sign up for this. I can't do this. This is beyond anyone's ability. It's ridiculous. You're ridiculous! I'm out of here.

You see, many people expect God to make them the star by using the battle plans they've developed and worked so hard on. We think of following God's lead as we think of following a football coach's directions. A good coach pushes you to do things that you are capable of but don't realize yet. They bring out your full potential. That's great, and God does that too ... but only after we have understood this first lesson. When you begin following Him, the battles are beyond any kind of skills you possess. Some battles will never be in our grasp. We can't win salvation or defeat Satan by our own strengths. Not now, not ever. This first lesson teaches us that our strength comes from God. He is our power source. Many of life's battles are not even ours to begin with. Consider this passage:

> **And that all this assembly may know that the Lord does not deliver by sword or by spear; for the battle is the Lord's and He will give you into our hands.**
> **—1 Samuel 17:47**

Notice the phrase "by sword or by spear." That basically means by our efforts and strengths. Hardship and dead ends are often the doorways in which God reveals Himself. What happens when we get angry at situations we can't handle and give up too quickly before God's point can be made? Look at the bind we put Him in! We want to know God is there waiting to tear down the walls of the impossible, but we won't push hard enough to even realize if something is impossible. If God tears down the walls too quickly, we credit ourselves.

As we return to the story in John 6 and examine it afresh, we find the apostles are standing before God with a problem. They look to their wallets first and realize they don't have the resources to buy food. They look to the crowd and realize that others can't offer any help. And so they stand before God Almighty and state, "It can't be done" (Ref. 5:1).

Once we understand the point He is trying to make, once we realize how impossible something is, only then does God move. He moves, and suddenly all things are possible. He crumbles the walls set before us, calms the storms, crushes the enemy we can't defeat, and in John chapter 6 He feeds thousands with two fish and five loaves.

At this point we have a choice. We can take the lesson to heart, or we can harden our hearts toward Him. The apostles chose the latter. In Mark's account, chapter 6 verse 52, we find the apostles had hardened their hearts and not understood the lesson behind the miracle of Jesus feeding five thousand. What does that mean? For the apostles it meant taking the class again, but the remedial class took place on a boat in the midst of a storm.

I can only guess at why the apostles hardened their hearts to the first miracle. I would guess they fell into the trap many of us do. We keep wanting God to increase our abilities. The apostles asked Jesus to *increase their faith*.

This is the process by which God increases faith. Oftentimes people ask God to strengthen their faith. They want to be stronger Christians, but many times their thinking is backward. They think becoming more faithful is becoming a stronger individual. That path would have people trusting more in their own abilities. God builds our faith by bringing us through the storm we are too weak to survive on our own. In this process we clearly understand our dependence on pulling strength from Him. Our faith increases when we understand our weaknesses. "*Increase our faith, God*" could be reworded as, "*Decrease my desire to look to myself, even when that means setting me against the impossible.*"

Now the words spoken to Paul make sense.

> And He has said to me, "My grace is sufficient for you, for power is perfected in weakness." Most gladly, therefore, I will rather boast about my weaknesses, so that the power of Christ may dwell in me."
>
> —2 Corinthians 12:9

He is the source of all good things and is life itself.

A few years after our marriage, my wife and I were presented with a new job opportunity at the church where I served as a youth minister. We had tried so hard to involve our teens and families in the community in Selma, Alabama. The elders wanted to branch into an evolvement ministry where I would serve as a community evangelist. The catch was I would have to raise money in order to have a salary, buy a bus, buy fund-raising equipment, and cover other new ministry costs like insurance and travel expenses. The congregation did not have the resources to help, but the desire to push forward to teach people was there.

After praying about this, we took the opportunity to do something we had never attempted before. I was trained by Ken Kilpatrick in Montgomery, Alabama. He was the director of the Montgomery Inner City Ministry and volunteered to help me understand fund-raising.

We set a budget and began working toward raising funds late in the year. In fund-raising you need to approach congregations in November while budgets are being set. Raising funds in the spring is very difficult. As April was nearing, we were about thirty-five thousand dollars short. That was about half the budget. The elders sat down with me to address the problem. The suggestion was made that we needed to cut, tighten, and rework everything in order to make ends meet. I couldn't stand the thought of cutting anything, because I had seen God pull me out of binds before. It's true that thirty-five thousand dollars was a lot more than that first five thousand for me to start college. And before, I was a single college student. I now had a wife to consider with our first child on the way. It was just that I hated putting "God" and "can't" in the same sentence.

"Let me go back home to Tennessee and raise funds there," was my request. Just give me a weekend to try to find more funding. They agreed, and I went back home to present the ministry and its needs. I spoke to four different congregations over the weekend, and they all were 100 percent behind this idea. I returned to Selma and reported how much I had raised. Would you like to take a guess at how much money I was able to raise in one weekend? Remember we needed only thirty-five thousand to make the budget. If you are thinking something big, you aren't following this chapter's thought process very well. :)

I raised zero in funds. The elders asked again, "What do you want to do?" The money is about to run out, and soon you won't have a paycheck. I wasn't sure what to say. I had no other place to turn. Within a week an anonymous donor from Birmingham sent a check to us through Ken for thirty-five thousand dollars. I never met the man, and I don't have any contacts in Birmingham ... but God does. Over and over I have seen Him do the impossible, and each time it seems the stakes are higher. Faith is a front-row ticket to watch God do amazing things! And in my efforts (my weakness), my faith has become stronger.

Prayer

Father and God, I stand before you as Job did. I'm frustrated and I'm discouraged, and that is putting it lightly. But I know all things are in your hands. Help me to focus on You instead of the storm. Help me smile, knowing the end of the story will reveal Your plan. Help me understand that impossible situations are where You often do Your best work. Give me strength to push forward in prayer although I can't see the path ... help me not break to this world.

Seek and Find

Simon Peter answered Him, "Lord, to whom shall we go? You have words of eternal life."
—John 6:68

Sometimes God lets you hit rock bottom so that you will discover that He is the ROCK at the bottom.
—Dr. Tony Evans

Often God allows us to break to keep us from being destroyed.
—Byron Smith

Chapter 6

Where Will You Meet the Stone?

The Box Parable

A man stands alone before God. He is smiling as he approaches a box. This box is a place of offering to God, a place where people give back to Him. It is apparent that this is a new concept to the man and he wants to start this relationship off on the right foot. With head up and hands toward heaven he asks, "What is it, Lord, that You want from me?"

God responds, "What do you want to give?" "I want to say thank You, Lord, for saving me", the man replies, "and I want to give to Your kingdom." The man pulls out his wallet. This was expected, and he came prepared. He holds out a hundred-dollar bill and drops it in the box. Touched, God responds, "Thank you so much. That will be a blessing to the hungry this month. I'm proud of you, son. This is a good start." The man was already returning his wallet to his pocket as the phrase "a good start" catches his attention. He brings his eyes back up to God's and asks, "Is this enough?" God responds, "Well, I'm sorry, but no, this isn't enough." The man begins to count out other large bills with a semi-concerned look on his face. As he slowly counts the bills, he tells God, "Just tell me 'when,' Lord." God is silent, and the man finishes counting the stack of cash and then just chucks his entire wallet in the box. God responds, "I am touched by your generosity. This is an amazing gift, and people in this city will be blessed by the work these funds will provide ... but if you are still looking to give enough, you aren't quite there."

The man looks taken back for the first time. This wasn't expected. "Lord, tell me what you would have me give. Would you like my car?" The man pulls the keys from his jacket and presents them as he continues, "It's practically brand-new with only eighteen thousand miles on it." He drops the keys in the box looking anxiously for a reply. God speaks again very gently, "Very few people have given so much back this early in their walk, and I'm so proud of you, but this still isn't enough."

At this point the man looks alarmed as he realizes this is more than he ever planned to let go. Desperately he checks himself and offers his watch. "Is it my time You want, Lord?" God responds, "Yes, I need your time as well." "How much will You require from me, God?" The man's voice strains under the pressure of what he is trying to give up. God responds, "How much do you want to give?" The man replies, "I want to give enough to make You happy." God responds, "Then I require it all."

At this point the man looks like he has just been slapped by a divine backhand. Please stop here at this scene, because this is what I will refer to as the "stone". This is the breaking point for so many people who are trying to follow God's lead. This is a critical decision we must make in our walk with God. The road forks, and we must choose a path.

Have you heard this voice? If not, spend the next month volunteering in a ministry to the homeless or abused. Get involved with a work focused around orphans and widows, or ask your congregation for a list of people who haven't been to church in a while and need encouragement. Follow that with a list of shut-ins. Ask if there are children at your church who need a positive

Christian presence in their lives. Trust me, you will hear this voice very soon. It's the voice of God calling upon His people to be His hands and minister to this world. The call is overwhelming. There are so many good ministries that will consume your life quicker than you think.

For those who are truly seeking to become more like Christ and not just "playing church," you will have to stand before this box. Playing church was exactly what the rich young ruler was doing. Don't judge him so quickly. He was a nice guy, a good person, and in Mark 10:21 the Bible tells us that Jesus looked upon him with love. Make no mistake about it. This was someone we would have all held up as a standard, a great humanitarian. But when he presented himself before the box, he faltered. Jesus told him, "If you want to be complete, go sell your possessions and give to the poor, and you will have treasure in heaven; and come, follow Me." Many casually point out his faults without stepping into his shoes. Keep growing as a Christian, and you will stand where he stood. And once you are there, you will choose one of two paths.

The first option is the path that the rich young ruler took. We get a little defensive. God has asked too much. I mean, look at all I am trying to do. I'm a good person and I'm trying to do my part, but what You are asking for is insane. The defensiveness turns to resentment. A bitter spirit overwhelms us as we consider our reasoning and we simply walk away. We can't find it in ourselves to give any more, and it simply hurts to stand before God knowing more is expected. Not wanting to be a failure, we simply quit. So many people choose this course of action, this mind-set. And they miss out on an amazing life.

The second option is where the man simply steps into the box himself. God is satisfied by the man's actions, and he finds peace in the fact that God is pleased. But that's not all. Once he steps into the box, he finds all the stuff he put in there. His time, car, and money are returned to him. So what was the point, you ask. Simply this: before, when the man was outside the box, everything was his. Now he realizes everything is God's. And when God has need of something, the man understands he is only a steward and follows faithfully. I'm not saying we can ever fully answer the overwhelming call of the harvest, but we make that harvest part of our life and mission.

> Jesus said to them, "Did you never read in the Scriptures, 'The stone which the builders rejected, this became the chief corner stone; this came about from the Lord, and it is marvelous in our eyes'? Therefore I say to you, the kingdom of God will be taken away from you and given to a people, producing the fruit of it. And he who falls on this stone will be broken to pieces; but on whomever it falls, it will scatter him like dust."
> —Matthew 21:42–44

Now, this passage directly addresses the Jews of the first century. Many rejected Christ as the Messiah, and many people today do the same. But I want to use the next part of this verse to address a wider audience.

The stone here is not just Christ, but also His teachings and His church. What I have referred to as "the box," scripture calls "the stone." Consider now the options we have when meeting the stone. You see, the first option in our verse is this:

And he who falls on this stone will be broken to pieces;

This is the option we need to take, the one where we step into the box. This is the moment in life when we follow God's voice, which leads to the breaking of our hearts, pride, and self-righteousness. This is where we meet the stone on this side of the grave. Imagine falling from a ladder that we designed and climbed like a pedestal.

We hit the stone ground hard, and it is not a comfortable experience. Breaking hurts, but it beats the alternative. If we decided to hold onto our own lives, then we are presented with the second option.

... but on whomever it falls, it will scatter him like dust.

Here the image is flipped, and in judgment the 'Stone' falls upon us. The verse describes our end result differently. We aren't broken then; we are instead crushed to dust. Either way, we will all meet the stone, also known as Christ and His teachings.

Understanding this lesson is essential before the true journey begins. So many people begin this Christian walk with our Savior, but they cannot continue the path because the stone stands in the way. They beat their heads against the stone hoping it will move, because it just doesn't make sense to them. They don't understand it is a doorway.

It's like a marriage. There is a "honeymoon stage" where everything is new. You are new ... new life, sinless, and in love with the Savior you've come to know. In marriage you hear the older generations say, "Enjoy the honeymoon phase." Later on when hard times hit, they say, "Looks like the honeymoon is over." Marriage isn't all eat, drink, and be merry, as we know. It gets tough, and compromises followed by sacrifices begin to take a toll on us. We slowly begin to lose self, and some people panic in this process. Being married to someone means becoming one with him or her. You both grow into something more. Yet people fight it, and when they can't fight anymore they run from it. The Bible teaches us that being baptized into Christ is like that wedding ceremony (Romans 6:3,4). We begin that walk with Him feeling excited and ready to follow Him anywhere. Then we meet the stone. Why, you ask. Why can't the marriage and the Christian life be a nice smooth ride? For many reasons.

You know how every once in a while you see an older couple still in love. You know the one I'm talking about … where the seventy-eight-year-old man with a walking cane is opening the car door for his wife. She doesn't smile at the moment. This isn't where you see the love, because she is tired and concerned about many things now. Keep watching, because later you find her wiping something off his face or adjusting his clothes. She accepts his gestures of respect and strength as he accepts her gestures of concern and care. He then reaches out to take her hand, and they push forward. This is where we see the love, where they have pushed through the hardships in life and been bonded on a deeper level. They have become one. In order to be the married couple who celebrate their fiftieth wedding anniversary, you have to make it through the fifty years of hardships.

In John 1:42 Peter is brought to Jesus and is given a new name. From the very start Peter feels the impact of Jesus's presence. In Luke 5:8 Peter realizes that he is standing before God, and he responds, "Depart from me, because I am a sinful man, O Lord." Yes, in this moment we see Peter humbled, but this isn't Peter falling and breaking on the stone. He only acknowledges that he isn't worthy to be in Jesus's presence, because he is a sinner. Peter's journey has so many ups and downs. In John chapter 6, Jesus gives a very powerful but misunderstood lesson. The Jews had very strict dietary laws, and Jesus tells them that anyone who follows Him must eat his flesh and drink his blood. Take a moment to read that chapter from the early Jew's perspective. There is a film called *The Gospel of John*; if you can locate the film, watch this chapter. Upon hearing this teaching we reach verses 60–68.

> **Therefore many of His disciples, when they heard this said, "This is a difficult statement; who can listen to it?" … As a result of this many of His disciples withdrew and were not walking with Him anymore. So Jesus said to the twelve, "You do not want to go**

away also, do you?" Simon Peter answered Him, "Lord,
to whom shall we go? You have words of eternal life."
—John 6:60, 66–68

The very characteristic that gets Peter in trouble so often is also
a quality I believe Christ loved about him. He spoke exactly what he
felt. There was no filter between his heart and his tongue. Here Peter
felt the stone in the teaching. He hadn't hit it yet, but he couldn't run
from it either. "To where would we go?" What a beautiful insight
into Peter's soul in that moment, as it foreshadowed things to come.

As we continue to watch Peter, we find him walking on water
and then sinking, being given the keys to the kingdom and then
referred to as Satan. Please note that Peter is saved through all this.
I want to be clear in what I'm saying about falling on the stone. This
isn't the point where we are saved; it's not the wedding ceremony
or honeymoon. It's the point where reality collides with our 'wants'
and it's sink or swim. Hitting the stone as I am presenting it is
comparable to the seed that fell on thorny ground in Luke chapter
8. The seed started to grow. Life was present, but then the roots were
'choked' by something and it could not reproduce. The Christian's
growth is stunted because he or she is overwhelmed with the thorns
of worldly desires. People want Jesus and a spiritual life is present,
but it is unhealthy. Notice the scriptures never say this seed dies or
perishes to the elements. But it cannot grow either, and therefore
God will cut it off. These seeds hit the stone I'm referring to—the
point where we stand before the box and realize just how much God
is asking for. We weigh Him against the world, or perhaps more
accurately stated, we weigh what we want against what He wants.

Now we come near the end of Peter's three-year internship, the
moment when he must choose. The account is found in Luke 22.
Read the whole chapter to really grasp this moment.

> "Simon, Simon, behold, Satan has demanded
> permission to sift you like wheat; but I have prayed for
> you, that your faith may not fail; and you, when once
> you have turned again, strengthen your brothers." But
> he said to Him, "Lord, with You I am ready to go both
> to prison and to death!" And He said, "I say to you,
> Peter, the rooster will not crow today until you have
> denied three times that you know Me."
>
> —Luke 22:31–34

So much takes place in this verse. First of all, notice this phrase, "when once you have turned again." Other versions use phrases like, "when you have turned back," and "when thou art converted." The words of Christ paint a picture of a life-changing moment coming for Peter—a "conversion," no less. This is an odd thought because we know Peter is already a convert and an apostle of Christ. How can a conversion take place now? And notice Satan will sift Peter like wheat through his hands. Peter is about to be run through the mill by Satan, and in the process a deeper relationship with God is coming.

Of course, Peter claimed he would never deny Jesus. And he was sincere in this gesture. Remember it was Peter who drew his sword and attacked a squadron of Roman soldiers. He was then rebuked by Christ and told to put his sword away. It was also Peter who followed Christ at a distance and tried to at least be there for Jesus in case He changed His mind and wanted to fight.

Peter was ready to die for Christ, but that wasn't what was asked of him. Peter, along with all of us, was asked to live for Christ. Or to rephrase this, we aren't asked to die physically; we are asked to die spiritually (Galatians 2:20).

As we close on Peter's experience, we can easily compare him side by side with Judas. Both betrayed Christ. Both were consumed with guilt and sorrow. Peter caught the eyes of Christ as he finished denying Him and ran off to weep bitterly. Judas threw the silver coins at the feet of the priest and claimed he had betrayed innocent blood. They both stood before the stone. They both threw themselves down. One was broken upon the rock, and one was stopped short by a rope. Judas could not get over himself. He could not get past his own pride and therefore could not fall upon the stone. Instead he chose to let the stone fall upon himself in judgment.

The stone is the point in our Christian walk where we understand what "dying to self" and living for Christ really means. Yes, we are a Christian upon obeying the Gospel the same as we are married when we say "I do." But to think that in sixty seconds I have become one flesh with my wife *perfectly* is folly. I've been married now for eighteen years, and I'm still learning to become one with her. This stone is the first doorway into that deeper walk with Christ. People wonder why the Bible states that the Straight and Narrow is the gate that enters into life, and *few there be who find it.* It's because so many people who have known Jesus still turn back to their old flame of *self.* They walk away from the box bitter or refuse to allow God to get too close.

Some refer to a statement, "Once saved always saved." This thought or teaching leaves the idea that people can never walk away from God after they have become Christians. And if people do turn away from the truth and go back to the world, they claim the person was never "saved" in the first place. I don't see this in scripture. Consider Paul's statement below:

> Do you not know that those who run in a race all run, but only one receives the prize? Run in such a way that you may win. Everyone who competes in the games exercises self-control in all things. They then do it to receive a perishable wreath, but we an imperishable. Therefore I run in such a way, as not without aim; I box in such a way, as not beating the air; but I discipline

my body and make it my slave, so that, after I have
preached to others, I myself will not be disqualified.
—I Corinthians 9: 24–27.

Sin has no power to pull me away from God's grace, but I could
still choose to walk away from Him because I'm done struggling
to run the race. If turning away from God after being saved and
becoming disqualified to claim the prize is not possible, then why
does Paul make this statement? Just as God intended marriage to
last a lifetime, He intends your covenant with Him to last as well.
He accepts us for "better or worse" as long as we continue to walk
with Him and wrestle against the flesh. As Paul puts it, we have no
reason to fear the security of God's promise. We simply get up when
we fall and push forward. Some, like the rich young ruler and Judas,
just refused to push that far forward.

As we end this chapter, we begin to shift gears in this book. The
"seek and find" lessons have been discovered, and I'm not saying
they are over by any means. But as we turn this page, new lessons
are presented: lessons of "Be Still and Know I AM God" or perhaps
"Be Still and Remember that I AM God."

Along with this chapter prayer, I want to share the thoughts of
this poem. I wrote it as a reflection of what Peter may have written
as he found himself falling on the stone or *God's will*. Hopefully, this
can direct your thoughts as you enter your talk with God.

Prayer

Lord God, Creator of all things wonderful and beautiful, help
me see past my own desires and wants. I empty myself before
You, and all I have is Yours. Help me to step into that box
so that You have complete control. Help my mind to join my
spirit there and begin to mold and shape me as You desire.

THE NAILS

Lord I was honored to stand by You today
As You poured out Your heart so people might be saved
And I asked You that moment "Please bless me with"
The ability to touch people's hearts as You did.

And I saw You again while vanishing their worries
By showing them signs of God's awesome glory
I asked You then "Please grant me that too"
And help me to be every day more like You.

I saw how You put the scribes to shame
While answering their questions of Your holy name
And I asked once again "Please give me a mind"
That I may answer things of future times.

I promised that "I will not deny You"
And though all were offended I would be true
But when You went to the cross to suffer all hell
I could not bring myself to ask for the nails.

'Be Still and Know'

My soul, wait in silence for God only, For my hope is from Him. He only is my rock and my salvation, My stronghold; I shall not be shaken.
—Psalm 62:5–6

Sticks and stones are hard on bones, aimed with angry art, words can sting like anything but silence breaks the heart.
—Phyllis Mcginley

I don't want to be in a battle. But waiting on the edge of one I can't escape is even worse.
—Pippin, Return of the King

Chapter 7

The Silence

It is an amazing concept how silence can be deafening, such as when a question goes unanswered: *"Do you still love me?"* or *"Are we going to be okay?"* When replies do not come and we are left in limbo to ponder every possible reason or outcome, silence becomes a paralytic fire that consumes our thoughts. This isolation of the soul and mind is one of the worst mental experiences we must endure.

Darius Rucker's hit "I Got Nothing" sums up silence in a powerful way. In the music video, a man's marriage is on the verge of divorce and the wife wants to hear that he still cares. The husband is silent. He wants to say something, his soul is crying out to give her the words she needs, but the body and mind are numb and unresponsive. And as much as I hate the concept, I love the song and video. It captures a moment that we know, fear, and to which we can relate.

I recall a story Jerry Clower used to tell, about a man who waited on God. A man lived in a valley that had been developed by the construction of a large dam. One day the dam cracked and water began to pour through and flood the valley in which many lived. A police boat pulled up to the man's house. The floodwaters already were rushing over the front porch. The owner sat in his porch swing and greeted his would-be rescuers. "Good day, officers. Can I help you?" "Sir," the officer replies, "we believe it is only a matter of time now before the dam breaks and water covers this valley. Get in the boat now and let us save you." The man replies in a deep God-fearing tone, "God's gonna take care of me! Get on out of here with your boat, because I know I'll be fine. God has never failed me, and I don't believe for a moment that He plans to start today." The police leave and continue their rescue operation.

Four hours later another boat comes up. It's a bigger boat, stronger and with more gear. The waters are covering the house up to the roof now, and the man is stranded there sitting on the shingles. "Sir, the dam did break. There's no hope now. Come on and get in the boat. Let us save you." The man replies, "Did you not understand me before? God is gonna take care of me. You think a little thing like a dam breaking will sway my faith? Leave me alone, and go help those who need you."

An hour later the waters have covered the home. The man is standing waist-deep on his chimney. The police hover in with a rescue helicopter. They drop down a rope ladder, and over the loudspeaker they plead with the man, "Sir, please grab on and climb up. You are going to die if you don't allow us to save you." "Get out of here with your fancy flying contraptions. God's gonna take care of me."

So the man dies. As he stands before the throne of God, he bites his tongue and shuffles around. "What's wrong?" God asks. "Well, Lord, I'm a little upset. You made me look like a fool. I thought you were gonna take care of me." "You dummy," replies the Lord. "I sent you two boats and a helicopter" (Ref. 7:1).

What does silence do to a person? In this illustration the man should have moved instead of remaining still. Silence often produces irrational responses and the constant struggle of answering the question of when or even if to take action. As we turn our minds back to scripture, this concept rings true in some different ways.

Abraham was promised a son by God. Then God was silent on the topic for twenty-five years. He promised in Genesis 12:4–5 to make Abram's descendants into a great nation. Then in Genesis chapter 21 at the age of one hundred Abraham sees that promise fulfilled. The only problem is that Abraham had given up on waiting years earlier and had taken another wife, Hagar. You could write a book on the ways the descendants of Isaac and Ishmael have fought, even to this day and age, but that is another lesson. I want to look at those first few years of waiting. What does silence do to one who is waiting on God, who tries to be still and know?

Abraham had a lot of time to think, and I can almost hear the thought process play out. *God promised me a son, but it's been a while. Am I supposed to do something? Is God waiting on me? Have I missed a door He's opened? Have I missed a sign or message given? Lord, please give me direction; please show me what You want me to do.* I don't believe Abraham doubted God as much as doubted his own role. Did *I* miss something? If you want an illustration, just tell your child that you have a present that you plan to give him or her. Make sure the child sees the gift beautifully wrapped and lying there. Instruct the child to go on about the day as normal and that later he or she can have it. You never told the child when or even what day he or she would receive the gift, but watch how often the child will come around and ask questions like, "Is there anything else I need to do?" You never said the child had to complete a certain deed, but after a small amount of time passes the child begins wondering why he or she hasn't received the gift. The child doesn't doubt the gift's existence but begins to wonder how to help the process move along to the "getting" part, because, "Why should I have to wait?"

Now enters Sarah with a bright idea, "*Take Hagar and have a child.*" I can almost hear Abraham's mind working: *Is this Your will? Is this a sign? Are you speaking Your will through the lips of my wife? It makes sense, and I don't want to assume God has to answer me in only ways that I see fit. Who am I to tell God how He needs to fulfill His promise?* Bottom line: I don't want to miss the "two boats and a helicopter."

The silence is a time we fear; it is the calm before the storm where we can only anticipate what is coming. It's the moment of choice when the question comes. Am I to seek and find a way to push forward or be still and wait on God? Most of the time, we choose to move. Why? Simple—it's because we hate waiting, especially when the waiting room is ground zero for life's trials and heartaches. It is by far the harder road.

Examine the following verse:

> But Moses said to the people, "Do not fear! Stand by and see the salvation of the LORD which He will accomplish for you today; for the Egyptians whom you have seen today, you will never see them again forever. The LORD will fight for you while you keep silent."
> —Exodus 14:13–14

Moses tells the people to be still and watch God's salvation. You can picture Moses standing nine feet tall and bulletproof. Staff in hand, he is ready for anything, right? Now read the next verse:

> Then the LORD said to Moses, "Why are you crying out to Me? Tell the sons of Israel to go forward."
> —Exodus 14:15

Why does God ask Moses to stop whining about what will happen when he just told the people to be still and watch God's wonders? You have to wonder how much time has passed within those verses. An hour? Four hours? As Moses and Israel wait, they look upon their enemies encamped behind them, pinning them against the sea. How long does it take a man of faith like Moses before he starts asking, "Could you hurry this plan up, God? I've told the people you are going to really dazzle them this time … you are going to dazzle them, right?" Moses must have heard his own words echoed back over the years to come as he led this impatient people to the promised land: "So are we there yet?" "I'm hungry." "I don't like this; I want something else." "Why is it taking so long?"

So how do we deal with the silence? How do we stand firm instead of bolt? That answer comes from God, because even in His silence we can hear answers if we listen.

You must understand that God views silence differently than humans. Humans ultimately view silence as abandonment. This is because we, like children, want our parents' attention in a certain way. Consider how often toddlers cry out for attention. Have they been forgotten in the backseat? No, the fact that they are in the backseat on a road trip is evident that they have not been forgotten. And sometimes those road trips are entirely focused around the children.

Still, that doesn't help the child in the backseat. The child still desires the attention, and the parent still has to drive the car. Is there any peace or comfort to be given? I believe so.

My wife would sometimes sing or talk softly to give comfort. And it comes in a small still voice that may not be the touch or attention we wanted, but to refuse to hear that voice is foolish. To reject the comfort given because it's not the comfort we wanted is childish. Older children can exaggerate the point and say they have been abandoned and forgotten. Oh, what dramatic and emotional creatures we are. How does this point apply to God? We must ask whether God is ever truly silent.

> **The heavens proclaim the glory of God. The skies display his craftsmanship.**
>
> **—Psalm 19:1**

Often, God's silence should be viewed more like teachers' silence on the topic they love. The restraint from speaking is their attempt to help us learn. They know that we have to discover some answers for ourselves in order to appreciate them. This same principle applies at camp when I am asked to run rope-course challenges. The key to running these team events is not giving the direct answers on how to complete the challenges. If you do, you ruin the events, the team building component, and the visual lessons.

Sometimes God's silence is that of parents. They can't tell the child, because, frankly, the child doesn't have the maturity to understand. And so parents simply try to give the child some encouragement.

In times of silence, God gives his people comfort. Now, many will argue with this, claiming that they don't feel comforted. The illustration carries through as we observe the ten-year-old who has a minor bike accident. This is no longer a toddler. He has grown into boyhood. The father may not run to the child's side to pick him up like when he was three. He may stop the mother from running to kiss the boo-boo on her son's knee. Instead he calls to him from a distance, "You're okay, buddy. Get up and try it again." We understand that it's not because we don't care or love them anymore, but that learning to get up and try again is something they must grasp. Allowing your children to learn from their mistakes and be silent as they are making them is tough.

No matter what is happening in our lives, we can hear that steady voice. All around us God's creation screams out that He is here and He cares. We need to see God's silence for what it is. Calling it abandonment isn't fair. Instead we have to take comfort in the fact that we are still here. As long as this world remains and time exists, hope exists. As long as God allows us more time, the road trip isn't over and judgment hasn't come. We have time to get our lives in order, tell our loved ones to do the same, and give Him something back from the life we've been given.

Some still want to complain that God doesn't comfort. Let me be straightforward then. God's comfort comes in many ways. The Holy Spirit was sent to be a "Comforter." The Holy Spirit through inspired men gave us the Bible, aka the "Words of Life."

How many hurt and yet refuse to take comfort in His Word? They send up the prayers like clockwork, but that's only half of the conversation. They expect the Father to pull over and crawl in the backseat with them instead of simply taking comfort from His Word. (Please understand in an emergency He may, but that's closer to the end of the book. And His definition of emergency differs from our own.)

Often our own children are echoes of our God's voice. I believe God designed this to show us and teach us the position of a parent. We should write down all the things we tell our children and hear God's wisdom behind those statements.

"You will see when we get there. You won't even think about the road trip then."

"We will get there when we get there"." How can you explain time to a three-year-old?

"It's a surprise." Because even if you explained this destination, words wouldn't give it justice and telling just leads to more questions.

"Because I said so." When the child forgets who runs the home and wants no part in helping with the household duties.

And finally my favorite, *"Trust me. Have I ever tried to hurt you?"* Even if they fall and hurt themselves while trying to learn new skills.

Now, I know there are some extreme examples still hanging within some of you: abuse, abduction, or sexual crimes. Those are difficult topics, and when discussing them, people who have been affected become defensive.

When I am approached by teens who are requesting help, they sometimes describe terrible situations. I often find myself listening to a lot of detail about many different people who have mistreated them. I acknowledge their pain, but then I have to ask what their intent is. Are they looking for answers, or are they looking for someone to condemn their offenders? I am only able to help them with choices and decisions within their control.

They protest that this person has done wrong. True, but neither God nor I is in control of their choices. And again, I explain if they are looking for help, I can only guide them within what is in their control. I can listen to problems and pray God humbles the third parties. (I'm sure that is already being done.) But like Pharaoh, some will harden their hearts until the end.

It is in these moments that we take comfort in God's holiness instead of His love. God is just, and some find this thinking unhealthy. I would point out that God has given many pictures of this in scripture. So many cry out to God for justice. There is a correct way and a wrong way to do this. Scripture has asked that when we turn to Him with these extreme problems, we cast those cares upon Him so that He might sustain us.

> **Cast your burden upon the LORD and He will sustain you; He will never allow the righteous to be shaken.**
> **—Psalm 55:22**

The idea here is to bring those problems to God so we can draw strength and comfort from Him. Some are burdened with situations that bring so much grief, and they are waiting for God to act. Often we don't hand those burdens over to Him. We can't let them go until we see that justice has been dealt. So we just walk beside Him pointing out the burdens we are carrying and demand that something be done. No relief can be given, because nothing has been let go.

Prayer

Lord, I praise you, even during the silence. I know you are aware of my life and the issues I face. Dear Father, I place those cares and burdens with You. Just knowing You are in this with me, directing my life quietly, gives me comfort. Help me be content and patient, but above all strengthen me through the storm.

'Be Still and Know'

But they that wait upon the LORD *shall renew their strength; they shall mount up with wings as eagles; they shall run, and not be weary; and they shall walk, and not faint.*

—Isaiah 40:31

Don't try to rush things that need time to grow.

—Unknown

Learning how to be still, to really be still and let life happen —that stillness becomes a radiance.

—Morgan Freeman

Chapter 8

Be Still ...

All my life I see God leading it. I see in hindsight the way God prepared me for the work I am doing now. In 2011 I was serving in my fifth year at Gulf Coast Bible Camp. I had wanted to help refurbish this place that meant so much in the lives of young people. God blessed the efforts, and here I am looking at the near completion of many of the projects we set out to accomplish. So I know God is with me, but in the last four years his voice has grown silent, still leading, still opening doors, but silent in direction on where I'm heading.

After the first year at camp, my wife and I decided to sell our home in Mobile, Alabama. It took me about fifty minutes to drive out to the camp. That was an hour and forty minutes of travel to go out and work at the campground. As I became more involved, the more trips I needed to make. Staying for several retreats and camp sessions was becoming harder. It seemed like I was watching my wife bring up our children alone. Some board members wanted me at even more events, and I kept waiting for God to open a door to move, but nothing opened. After four years of waiting, the economy hadn't improved at all. I was ready to move the family to the camp so we could work there together, and yet no opportunities presented themselves. God was silent.

It's so frustrating to be led by God and hear His voice, and then to feel left in silence longing to hear that voice again. I want reassurance that I'm still on the right path; I want to know what will be ahead for my family next year. Should I buy a house and move to Lucedale, Mississippi, nearer to the camp? I could. I could try to rent my current house and just trust that God will provide. I could purchase a new home in Mississippi and take on a second mortgage, but would that be trusting God's provisions or failing to trust His timing? Do I "seek and find" or "be still and know"?

Join me as we revisit the story of Israel's first king. Step in his shoes for a moment. In I Samuel 13 Saul has been called to play the role of king. He is about to lead his army to war with the Philistines and is waiting for Samuel the prophet to arrive. This is a big moment for Saul. In the previous chapters, he has heard God's call, seen visions, prophesied, and been anointed king of Israel. With war upon him, he waits impatiently on the old prophet, wanting direction from God. Samuel is late, and Saul, wanting to hear God's voice again, panics.

> Now he waited seven days, according to the appointment time set by Samuel, but Samuel did not come to Gilgal; and the people were scattering from him. So Saul said, "Bring to me the burnt offering and the peace offerings." And he ordered the burnt offering.
> —I Samuel 13:8–9

This was forbidden. Only the priests were involved with offering sacrifices on the behalf of the people. Saul was not a priest or a Levite. He had no authority, as Samuel did, so why did he do it? Desperately, Saul chooses his path. He offers sacrifices himself to the Lord, although the place isn't his. Samuel arrives on the scene in disbelief of Saul's actions. Can you see the dilemma as it unfolds? Taste his frustration with God because he wants guidance. In his mind, time had run out and a choice had to be made. Desperate to hear God's voice, he pushes forward with nothing on his mind but his own time frame. In chapter 15, Saul is instructed to kill King Agag and utterly destroy the Amalekites. Again Saul "edits" God's command. Why? Verse 20 gives some insight into Saul's thoughts. He could have reasoned, *Why waste these perfect animals when they would make beautiful sacrifices? During the celebration feast of victory we will lift up the first one hundred lambs on the altar. As we offer sacrifices to God, everything eventually dies. I can make God's commandment work better!*

After this account, Samuel tells Saul that God will take his kingdom away and give it to a man after His own heart. Saul now faces going into battles wondering whether or not God is leading the way. He is blind rushing into battles that may turn out in defeat. God is angry with him, and for a while he wants to hide from God. But where can he go? God's voice and presence have departed, and for a moment he's glad. Saul fears standing in the presence of an angry God. But as time passes, he second-guesses every decision. He doubts the path he chooses and then decides to just sit when he shouldn't. I see his dilemma more clearly as the story of David and Goliath unfolds only two chapters later. How can Saul respond to the challenge of Goliath? Go out to battle him without God's presence? *This may be God's way to end my reign; Samuel did say my kingdom would not endure and that God would appoint someone else to my throne. Is this the day? And if so, do I simply go and die so that God may judge me in my present state? I need more time* is the likely response to his inner thoughts. Something had to change, anything. And in his desperation *David walks in.*

As months roll on and years go by, the silence Saul experiences becomes unbearable. It's a silence that we all have heard from loved ones, but magnified times a thousand. It is tasting God's presence in your life and now dying slowly without it. I don't care if it's a small still voice of a calm shepherd or the wrath of a warrior God seeking vengeance. "Speak, Lord! I'm dying to just hear your voice again." It's this deafening silence that leads him to a witch in I Samuel 28. Reading Saul's life afresh has been more insightful with these thoughts in mind.

Now, don't think God is silent only when we've sinned. That's not the case at all. There is another story to consider in this passage. Remember when "David walks in" where we find Saul unable to make a decision? Some think that a king sending a teenage boy into battle to decide the fate of Israel is far-fetched. I don't, because as we have discovered, silence drives us to do crazy things. In this case we find an encouraging thought. Sometimes those crazy things may be exactly what God wants. In this case David is presented to Israel for the first time. The point could be made that a window of opportunity opens to David because of the silence Saul experiences as king.

There is one last account in scripture before we leave this thought, a story that has always stuck with me like a thorn in the back of my mind. The account is found in I Kings 13.

The story is about an old prophet and a younger one. This younger prophet was sent by God to send a message to His people and the king of that time, Jeroboam. The message isn't a good one, and the king doesn't like it at all. When Jeroboam tries to seize the man, his hand is withered and the altar splits apart allowing the ashes on it to be poured out. The king asks that the prophet pray to God for the sake of his hand. He does, and God restores the hand of the king. Jeroboam now entreats the man to stay at his house for the evening, which begins the part of the story I want to focus on.

> **But the man of God said to the King, "If you were to give me half your house, I would not go with you, nor would I eat bread or drink in this place. For so it was commanded me by the word of the Lord, saying, 'You**

shall eat no bread, nor drink water, nor return by the
way which you came.'"

—I Kings 13:8

So the man departs from the king. In that same area, an old
prophet now lived. His sons came and told him about the events that
had unfolded with the man of God and the king. The old prophet
quickly chased after the younger one and caught him on the road out
of town. He asked the young man to come home with him and eat
bread. The man of God told the old prophet the same thing, that God
had commanded him not to do so. In verse 18 we continue the story.

> He said to him, "I also am a prophet like you, and
> an angel spoke to me by the word of the Lord, saying
> 'Bring him back with you to your house, that he may eat
> bread and drink water.'" But he lied to him. So he went
> back with him, and ate bread in his house and drank
> water. Now it came about, as they were sitting down
> at the table, that the word of the Lord came to the old
> prophet who had brought him back; and he cried to the
> man of God who came from Judah, saying, "Thus says
> the Lord, 'Because you have disobeyed the command
> of the Lord, and have not observed the commandment
> which the Lord your God gave you, but have returned
> and eaten bread and drunk water in the place of which
> he said to you, "Eat no bread and drink no water"; your
> body shall not come to the grave of your fathers.'"
>
> —I Kings 13:18–22

After the man of God left, a lion attacked and killed him on
the road. I wonder now if the attack took place at the same point
where the young prophet had turned to go back with the older one.
Nevertheless, word came to the old prophet of what had happened
and that the lion remained standing by the body. The old prophet

went again, found the body, saw the lion standing by, and collected the body of the man of God. He then returned home and buried the man in his own tomb.

I never liked this passage much. Two things stood out. Why punish the younger man for an honest mistake? He had trusted someone that God had spoken through in times past. He may have even heard his name and was honored to meet him. Second, why did the old prophet have to do this? He had been in those shoes, understood the importance of following God, the seriousness of the commands He gave. So why on earth deceive the prophet and change commands given to him for apparently no good reason at all? What profit was there in this course of action? I think it was the simple thirst to hear God again.

I'm seeing this passage clearer than before. I'm sure that, like for all scripture, there is yet deeper meaning to be found, but at the moment the lesson is clear. We can't stand waiting for anything. We know He's there. There is undeniable proof that greater forces are at work in the creation of this universe, the world, and the human body. If you've ever read through a book on apologetics or Christian evidences, then you understand this statement. I know God's there; and that's the reason I long to draw near Him. The issue here is times when God is silent on the topic we feel is most important. We are driven to the point of making rash decisions out of impatience or making no decisions trapped by fear. We want to be on the right path but we can't hear Him, and so we aren't sure. Why can't He give us a heads-up? There are so many answers, but they come down to a general thought. It's not because we've done anything wrong; it's simply because it's not His time. Oh, how we hate this answer in our personal lives. We forget how much the answers impact us down the road. We forget how silence is able to magnify the acts of God. Sometimes silence has to play its part before we can even get a glimpse of God's intent.

The resurrection of Lazarus is one of the highlights of miracles performed by Jesus in the Gospels. Here we find silence paving the way again as it sets the scene. John 11:2–17 tells us that Mary and Martha sent word to Christ, but He stayed still. Silence was the only answer they received through Lazarus's last days and even four days afterward. And then silence breaks. God speaks, and the lessons are even more powerful. Jesus was not only in command of the physical world; He could reach beyond it! And suddenly the *silence* makes perfect sense.

Years ago, I had the opportunity to help with a Lads to Leaders program at church. A friend asked if I was interested in helping with speech. Some of our young men were preparing speeches for the convention, and I felt I could really be used in this way, so I signed up. One young man named Tim came to the second session. I'd never really met him, just seen him in the halls a few times. Tim didn't seem very interested in the whole idea at first. We had a one-on-one session for about twenty-five minutes, and I could see the wheels turning in his head. It's a great feeling when you can connect with someone so quickly. Everyone knows how it feels when you wish someone could just step inside your mind and see it from your point of view. Well, that's close to what Tim did. He worked hard on his speech, and I gave tips here and there. Over the next few weeks he completed it. I heard him deliver it at a small congregation down the road. He did well, but there were still some pointers to be made. His mother took him to a Toastmasters session and told me he picked up some more information.

A few weeks later I heard him give the speech again. It had been a month since the last speech was given at the little neighboring church. This time he was before a much larger crowd at our home congregation. I wasn't feeling well, so I was standing in the back of the auditorium. The following week he would be at the convention, and I wanted to hear him one more time to see if there was any more guidance to be given. He did a wonderful job. He was adding dramatic pauses and changes in tempo to maximize his effectiveness. He could still give the speech better, but as I concluded, he had all he needed ... at this point.

All the tools to put together a speech and deliver it were there. Now, that doesn't mean I still didn't see lessons I could share with him. I could see that he himself knew he could have delivered it better, and he may have been a little agitated beneath the surface at small mistakes or losing his place for a moment. I wanted to warn him about lessons I'd learned along the way like, we prepare and deliver our best and trust God does what He will with our service. Be careful not to get caught up in how you feel about the presentation. God works through the power behind His words, because that message is His, not yours. I noticed the same praise coming to him after the service that I once received at his age. The lessons on pride and stumbling blocks of praise are other lessons I could share with him. *Make sure to remember you are only the messenger; it isn't about you.* I saw the signs of things that could come, but those are lessons for another time. Tim was fourteen years old. He needed encouragement and praise. He wasn't ready for those lessons yet. It would take time and experience before he'd even see a need for those lessons. He couldn't grasp them yet. Then I realized the lesson God was teaching me.

Tim's story is my own. Four years I've waited for answers, frustrated because I didn't receive them. Time after time I was second-guessing my own thought process and fighting urges to move without seeing His hand at work. I was a thirty-four-year-old child in the backseat asking, "Are we there yet?" And I've been doing it for four years now. God's time is exactly that ... God's time. There are some lessons I'm not ready for yet; I've not matured enough.

The last four years I've seen as "just waiting" and not as "preparation." So instead of trying to look for ways to improve my talents by study or service, I've simply wasted time, waiting for a door to open. I have done this because I see myself as ready for the next step, and I don't even know what that step is. Maybe He is allowing me time to understand this concept and even time to write a book. (If you're reading this, I'm sure glad I started using the time instead of waiting and wasting it.) Sometimes we have more growing to do before we move on, and for the moment, I have all the tools I need to work at His camp and take care of my family. *Be still, Byron, and know that I AM God.*

I wrote this chapter first in 2010. Of course, I've tweaked it along the way, but now I want to close with this last paragraph. It's 2016 and many of those issues have been resolved, but other burdens have been presented. The best way I have found to deal with trusting God in future trials is simply considering how He worked out the previous ones. I believe this is the whole idea about all the detailed stories we find in scripture. Helping us see how God has always been faithful and true is a comfort given to us by the Holy Spirit.

Prayer

Holy Father, please help me at this point in my life. I feel so trapped by situations and expectations that are out of my control. I feel the need to move past these ordeals in my life, because all I see is time being wasted. So I ask You to help me see things from Your perspective. Allow me the insight to see opportunities to grow and draw closer to You while I'm waiting. Use me to impact the journey of others whether I see it or not. Give me the will to push forward, even though I only see my wheels spinning in place, because I trust You are moving things too large for me to grasp.

'Be Still and Know'

Are you the one who is to come, or should we look for another?

—John the Baptist

Many want the fairy-tale, but forget each fairy-tale begins with tragedy that must be endured. Cinderella's ball is meaningless without the rest of the story.

—Byron Smith

So do I, and so do all who live to see such times. But that is not for them to decide. All we have to decide is what to do with the time that is given us.

—Gandalf the Gray

Chapter 9

... And Know that I AM God

Be still and know that I AM God.

—Psalm 46:10

What an amazing verse this is. At times it brings great comfort. It's the foremost thought in my mind when I can escape the world for a moment and be still. It's the verse I cling to when I look out over the ocean. I've watched storms roll in on the coast as I stood a hundred feet off the shore on a sandbar with nothing around me but the waves. One of the most amazing sights I've ever seen was the rain pounding into the ocean all around me, the drops glimmering like pearls as they impacted the water. The rain was so heavy I couldn't see the world I'd left behind. And caught up in this moment I just wanted to pray and praise Him for allowing me to just stand there and know He is God.

Often we think of the "Be still and know" moments as the mountaintop experiences in our spiritual walks. I've stood on that peak as well, looking out over the world. And once there I've watched as eagles flew by beneath me. Looking down upon their backs put in perspective how far away from the world I had climbed, and in that solitude I just wanted to praise my God. These moments, as precious as they are, are too few, it seems.

At other times, the concept of "Be still and know" is anything but comforting. These are the times I'm standing on a different seashore and the storms of life crash about me. No longer are the raindrops dancing like pearls on the ocean; now the drops are voices demanding something from me. And the storms are so heavy I can hardly see God at all. In these moments the thought of "being still" haunts me. I don't want to be still, Lord. I don't have the strength to stand in this tempest's path. I need to move, leave, or just run. We feel trapped in a life we don't want to be in. The thought of having to remain in these moments and wait for God is gut-wrenching. It brings a sick feeling of being imprisoned with your frustrations as cell mates.

These are the moments I want to "seek and find." *Lord, open a door for me, please. I need an escape.* But nothing happens. *Lord, if you aren't giving me a way out, then please still the storm and take it away.* And still the storm remains. *"What do you want from me, God? What must I do to find shelter?"*

And the response comes, *Be still and know I AM God.*

These are the moments that make or break us. It is in these moments, when our hearts have failed us and we have no strength left to stand, that we must choose. Will I trust in God, or will I find an alternative route?

Many choose an alternate route. To find comfort they turn to a hobby, sports, or other forms of entertainment. They look to alcohol, drugs, pornography, or other sexual escapes ... an affair perhaps. Anything to forget about the storm will do, if only for a moment. Our mind-set becomes, *Well, if I'm stuck here, I might as well find some enjoyable way to pass the time"* or *"I might as well make the best of a bad situation and have a little fun."* Be careful, or you will miss the second part of the verse: "and know that I AM God." If we follow that thought process of *just enjoy the time*, we follow Satan's distractions and miss the most amazing moments of life God has in store for us.

The cell is dark; little light can find its way into the corners of John's prison. It's been weeks, and slowly, for the first time ever, the darkness around him penetrates his hopes. It's a slow process. The same thoughts that comforted him have become his tormentors ... thoughts about various moments in his ministry over the last few years. There were the followers who looked to him for answers, bold preaching to the Pharisees, and then standing firm in the truth when King Herod himself chose to defy God's commands. But those days are behind him, and imprisonment has left him second-guessing everything. Now he questions the memories. Did he get them right, or had he fooled himself? He preached the power of God in Christ, yet no powerful Christ had come to save him. Follow the account again as John teeters over the edge of despair in this silence.

> The disciples of John told him about all these things. John summoned two of his disciples and sent them to the Lord to ask, "Are you the one who is to come, or should we look for another?" When the men came to him, they said, "John the Baptist has sent us to you to ask, 'Are you the one who is to come, or should we look for another?'" At that time he cured many of their diseases, sufferings, and evil spirits; he also granted sight to many who were blind. And he said to them in reply, "Go and tell John what you have seen and heard: the blind regain their sight, the lame walk, lepers are cleansed, the deaf hear, the dead are raised, the poor have the good news proclaimed to them. And blessed is the one who takes no offense at me."
>
> When the messengers of John had left, Jesus began to speak to the crowds about John. "What did you go out to the desert to see—a reed swayed by the wind? Then what did you go out to see? Someone dressed in fine garments? Those who dress luxuriously and live

sumptuously are found in royal palaces. Then what did
you go out to see? A prophet? Yes, I tell you, and more
than a prophet. This is the one about whom scripture
says: 'Behold, I am sending my messenger ahead of
you; he will prepare your way before you.' I tell you,
among those born of women, no one is greater than
John; yet the least in the kingdom of God is greater
than he."

—Luke 7:18–23

Notice what scripture has to say about John in this account at
the end: "He was more than a prophet,", and "I say to you, among
those born of women there is no one greater than John." There is
no doubt about how great John the Baptist is, yet here we find him
doubting. God in his wisdom shares this one account where we see
the world trying to break John ... a picture of what happens when
we must be still in the storm.

Finally, John can't wait any longer and seeks an answer from
Jesus. "Are you the Christ? Or should I be waiting on someone
else?" Can you relate to his question? Have you been in his shoes?
Let this moment sink in, because we all are about to hear God's
answer. And if you aren't careful you will miss it. "Know that I
AM God!" I realize that's not the wording used, but it's the message
given. "The blind see, deaf hear, lame walk, dead are raised, and the
poor have the gospel preached to them." We see Christ reminding
John that He is God, and he came to fight a much bigger war than
the physical well-being of mankind. He came to fight for our souls
("Blessed is the one who takes no offense at me."). John's work is
done, and he is about to put the exclamation mark on the end of
his lesson with his life.

Some of you are thinking, *That's a terrible answer!* or *That's
not the way the story should have gone!* Why not? And who are
we to direct the story? I think John understood the answer and

took comfort in it. His soul was in the hands of God, and no one could touch it. Heaven was waiting, and one final chapter stood between him and eternity. John saw the answer and accepted it. He remembered who God is—the author and perfecter of faith!

Too many times when God answers "No" or "Not yet," we complain that He has said nothing. If we choose to believe His silence is not an answer at all, we feel God has not heard us nor does He care. Bitterness and despair take our hand, and we go find some addiction to submerge ourselves in. It's because we have left ourselves hopeless.

If we instead understand God's silence as an answer, we can take comfort in the fact that He has heard us and cares for us. It's not going to happen the way we want, but we have not been ignored. It's a faith thing that makes the difference and gives us hope. Our limited knowledge, plus our overactive imagination, makes faith a *must*!

I believe the "Be still and know that I AM God" lessons are the hardest lessons that we are presented with in life. I'm not saying all the "Be still" lessons end in despair. I am, however, inclined to say that these lessons are presented to more spiritually mature followers. Yes, they hurt and we long for a more glorified path in following Christ again. Yet these lessons in patience bring the greatest wisdom and rewards to those who endure.

Now, being heard is not the only comfort we receive as we endure the storm. Let me share one more before we close this chapter

> Even young people become worn out and get tired. Even the best of them trip and fall. But those that wait upon the Lord will receive new strength. They will fly as high as eagles. They will run and not get tired. They will walk and not grow weak.
>
> —Isaiah 40:30–31

This passage has so much depth to it. I've learned that I need to revisit it often when my heart has given out. Let me share a few thoughts with you here. First, the verse says even the strongest people will eventually "wear out." If everyone eventually gets tired and falls, then one thing is for sure: we can't depend on our own might (physical, mental, or spiritual abilities) to get us through storms. Eventually we will give out and perish. The verse tells us we must wait on the Lord, or be still and know. If we do this, He will give us new strength; God will lift us up like eagles.

Have you ever looked out into one of those really bad storms before and watched birds flying around? Of course not; birds can't fly in that kind of weather. They find shelter and wait the storms out. I know what you're thinking: *Wait a minute. You said we weren't supposed to just find our own shelter, or alternative peace. Just finding ways to avoid the storm was avoiding the lessons God had in store for us.* That's right, but the passage isn't talking about just any bird; it's talking about an eagle. You won't find eagles flying through storms either, so where are they when the storms come? Eagles, unlike regular birds, have such powerful wings they can climb to amazing altitudes. When bad weather moves in, these large birds move above the storm. They can actually just fly over them (Ref. 9:1).

Wait a minute, Byron. I've asked God to take away the storms, and He hasn't. You even said a moment ago that God often leaves the storm in place and simply says, "Remain." Yes, I did. But don't confuse taking the storm away for being lifted above it. These are two very different concepts, and understanding the difference between them helps you hear God more clearly.

God gives us strength to keep following. This comes only when we remember the process we see in John's life. You can't be still in the storm and find some addiction to distract you. You can't be still and waste time feeling sorry for yourself and accuse God of abandoning you. "Be still and know I AM God," and watch what strength is given when we wait upon the Lord.

Prayer

> *My God, my Father, I am asking you now to help me in this situation I'm in. This storm has outlasted my strength, and I don't see an end in sight. I need new strength. Help me to focus on Your presence in this storm. Strengthen me to endure it. And use me even while I'm in it. Minister to my family, please, and draw us all closer to You. Amen.*

'Be Still and Know'

You let captors set foot on our neck; we went through fire and water; then you led us out to freedom.

—Psalm 66:12

He went away a second time and prayed, "My Father, if it is not possible for this cup to be taken away unless I drink it, may your will be done."

—Matthew 26:42

Fireproof doesn't mean the fire will never come. It means when the fire comes that you will be able to withstand it.

—Fireproof (the movie)

Chapter 10

The Fire

Hananiah stood on the edge of an enemy encampment. He was nearly fifteen years old, just really starting life. His home had been taken from him. His parents could be dead; he didn't know for sure. His future was no longer in his hands; it lay instead with his captors. A soldier yelled something in his direction, but it was in a language he didn't understand. This only added to his foglike state. Looking back over the last week of his life, he hoped to awaken from a dream. But the dream continued as the solider jerked him back into reality by the arm.

As Hananiah returned to a makeshift tent for captives, he saw three friends. They didn't make eye contact. Perhaps they too were still in a daze, and looking into the eyes of a friend would only confirm their worst fears. A question hung in the air over all four of them, a question that could not be answered, only pondered over and over. "What will happen now?"

The next day the journey ended, and it brought them to a new place they must now call home. The soldiers were talking again as they looked over a large group of children, all about the same age as Hananiah. They divided them, and soon a man approached the group of boys that the four friends had been assigned to. He commanded them to come, and without resisting the young men followed.

Fear had subsided in some ways as what the future held began to unravel itself. A master who spoke their native language had been set over them. He was firm but understanding, the only person they had met in this place who seemed to sympathize with them in a small way. They were schooled each day, learning the culture, customs, and clothing of this new world. New names had been given to them in the language of this new nation. Hananiah heard the name his master chose for him. Would everything be taken away, even his name? As he and his friends pronounced their new names, no one made eye contact. It was easier to change if no one was watching you.

As weeks passed by, fears slowly faded for Hananiah. But as fear left, other emotions began to flood the boy. Bitterness and anger came in the form of questions. Why did this happen? Could his parents have foreseen this? Couldn't the nation he was from have fought back? Hananiah had been taught enough of his nation's history to know they were a mighty and proud people. They were chosen. They served the one true God, who had promised to make them a great nation, but this made no sense now. If such a God is real, where is He? Why has He let these things happen? Why is He silent?

One evening the master brought in delegates from the royal court. They were talking to the master of the school, and it seemed like something wonderful was happening. The friends watched, hoping for some good fortune to come their way. The last few months had been broken dreams and disappointments followed by grief. Food from the king's palace arrived within moments, and the master gathered the young men with a pleased look in his eyes. The king had selected this group of young men to train for positions within his palace. They were going to be given fine clothing and an education from royal tutors and scholars, and even their food would be the best the land had to offer.

Hananiah smelled the food before he saw it. A feast fit for a king had been laid out before him. A door had opened, and hope had entered. Life might not go as badly as he had first thought. His eyes scanned the table, and something twitched inside him. His parents had never let him eat many of these foods. His people had been commanded by God to eat only a certain diet. This food was forbidden by their Lord ... the same God that was nowhere to be seen. The same God that let all these terrible things happen to him and his friends. The same God who had been silent.

Hananiah looked up before he could stop himself, maybe because this was a breaking point. This meant crossing a line between who they were and who they were being called to become. Whatever caused the reaction, it seemed to simultaneously happen to each of the four friends. Their eyes met; their hearts felt as if they might rip if they didn't act. So once the feast began, Hananiah and his friends approached the master of the house.

They approached him in the broken language that they had been taught. Hoping that this would show respect for the nation they were in and therefore help their case, they pulled the man aside. "Master, may we speak with you?" Hananiah's friend Daniel took the lead and explained they could not eat this food. The master listened and turned to Hananiah. "Is this how you feel as well, Shadrach?" Shadrach, or Hananiah, agreed with Daniel. They explained the situation that they, Daniel, Shadrach, Meshach, and Abednego, were bound by their God not to defile their bodies with the food offered by the king. Their master was impressed. Most of the young men wouldn't think of trying to form a complete sentence in Babylonian yet, much less carry on a conversation. Again the master had compassion on them and allowed them a ten-day trial.

You know the rest of the story. It's found in the first chapter of the book of Daniel. These young men are in an unfathomable predicament. Most of us can't even pretend we understand the trials they faced. At most we can conjure up some fitting details like I have done here. What we do know is this is a story of God's silence. Shadrach, Meshach, and Abednego go another three years without hearing anything from God. Actually, we have no evidence that God ever interacted with them directly until Daniel 3. Now, please consider this.

They could have easily seen their story differently. Abandoned by God while favored by the king could have been their view on their situation. Giving the king or the master credit while God was silent makes perfect sense from a worldly standpoint. But this isn't what they choose to see. For the next three years the same options are given. They continue to choose to see God's blessings in their lives.

What are these blessings? Good health, intellect, good looks. All these things people would normally credit to themselves and still complain to God about His lack of involvement. These young men choose to hear God even during the silence. After three years the plot thickens. Daniel goes on to even greater things in the king's services and appoints his friends as province officials within the government. As time goes on, King Nebuchadnezzar sets up a massive idol and calls for his subjects to bow down to it.

I don't know how much time has passed. I don't know where Daniel was or why the king would have made such a foolish decision. What we do see is how sometimes the same storm can roll back around even worse.

Hananiah (Shadrach) finds himself again hearing only the silence of God. This time the stakes are much higher, as they are brought in before the king himself in Daniel chapter 3.

The king is outraged with their refusal to bow to his will. He brings them in and questions them in person, thinking that in his presence their confidence would shatter. I can envision him in verse fifteen as he draws himself up to his full measure.

I'm going to give you one last chance to obey. When you hear the music play, bow down or I will destroy you within the fiery furnace. And what God out there can save you from my hands?

Instead of producing fear, that last remark from King Nebuchadnezzar hits a heartstring within these young men. "*What God, you ask?*" You have to appreciate this response given in the presence of the fire:

> **We are not careful at all on how to answer you in this matter. The God who we serve can deliver us, but even if he chooses not to we will not bow down to this image.**

At this point God is still silent. Shadrach, Meshach, and Abednego witness the full wrath of the king's rage. They have stood firm yet again, and still God does not speak. They hear the commands for the furnace to be cranked up, and still God doesn't move. They are devoured by the soldiers who are hoping to appease the king by their quick and brutal response in binding them. Still there's nothing from God. They have just enough time to think it over as some of the soldiers themselves die in the flames prepared for them. And finally they are carried helplessly to the fire's entrance and thrown—

Stop right there on *thrown*. Don't go any further. We all know what happens, and we long to rejoice with them, but don't rush so quickly to the end that you miss this part of the account. They were thrown into a fiery furnace. I imagine how that moment felt. Dragged all the way to this nation years before, all my life doing my best to follow God, and here at the end He has chosen to let me die looking like a fool. At this point you brace yourself for what's next. You prepare to burn. I will feel the fire, the pain, and then death. They did not waver in their faith, because they knew God was with them, *even while He chose to remain silent.* So many of us feel like we are watching the fire's preparation in our own lives. We see how events are leading us in a direction we don't want to go. How do I know God will be with me through the fire?

They knew because they had always seen God providing the blessings in their lives. They had heard His voice in His blessings no matter how small they were. How can you hear His voice when heartaches are so deafening that all hints of hope are drowned out?

Terry Cagle is a friend who shared an amazing story on God's silence and provision. He and his wife, Michelle, were struggling with the fact that no matter how hard they tried or prayed, she could not conceive. After waiting for years, they decided to try some other options. Artificial insemination attempts at pregnancy cost the couple about twenty thousand dollars. Just so you know, Terry is the minister at the Azalea City Church of Christ in Semmes, Alabama. Preachers don't have twenty thousand dollars just lying around. It hurts to lose that kind of money. The attempts were not fruitful, and they finally accepted that this door had been shut by God as well.

Consider that moment. God puts within us a desire to have children, and he stops us from having one in every direction we proceed. How discouraging is it to push forward in faith, to seek and find and spend twenty thousand dollars praying God will reward your faith and make a way? Instead, the answer comes back no, and now you have another problem instead of a blessing—twenty grand in debt. How easy would it be to blame God or reject His existence altogether?

Later Michelle did conceive, and Terry had another choice. How do you view this turn of events? He simply said, "God turned His no into Bo" (the name of their first child). Here is an interesting fact about the story, though. The twenty thousand dollars spent didn't ruin them financially. God provided ways to help them through their efforts even while He was saying, "No, that is not what is going to happen right now."

God providing in the silence is often His words of comfort. Even when we are pushing opposite to the direction He has in mind, He gives us comfort and sustains us. When you find God is providing a way for you and protecting you in the midst of the storms, chances are you may need to be still and continue to wait on God. But even if we continue to push, don't think God will be angry with you or think that He doesn't understand. Just make sure you continue to respect His answer, hear Him through those small but immensely important blessings. They are like a whisper to a child in the dark, "I know it's dark, but don't focus on the darkness … Focus on Me." If God has opened no doors and instead ministers to your needs as they arise, what do you think He's saying?

Thoughts for your prayer

To understand God in this way requires one to be broken. After some thought, I'm not sure I can help you start a personal prayer like this. I encourage you to lay everything out before God … let all the pain and questions you have fall upon Him, not for answers, but just to unload that burden upon His shoulders. Remember who it is that hears you, and know He cares.

'Pressing Forward in Stillness'

These things I have spoken to you, so that in Me you may have peace. In the world you have tribulation, but take courage; I have overcome the world.
—John 16:33

She stood in the storm, and when the wind did not blow her away, she adjusted her sails.
—Elizabeth Edwards

To die will be an awfully big adventure.
—Peter Pan

Chapter 11

Untouchable

Have you ever considered the prayers we lift to God? What are some of the things we pray for?

"Lord, help me with this situation I'm in!"

"Lord, watch over my family and keep them safe."

"Lord, take away the temptations that ensnare me."

"Lord, I ask You to deliver me from this pain."

"Father, humble those who have set themselves against me and have broken my will to stand."

Many of our prayers are asking God to help us become "untouchable" as far as this world goes. We don't want to be vulnerable. We seek to be immune from the stresses of this world, the heartaches that engulf us in sorrow. We look for an escape from pain and physical suffering. We desire it, sing about it, search for it, and then pray God gives it. So please consider with me for a moment what the answer to that prayer would look like.

If your children are scared of the dark, how do you help them? If they fear the water, how can they overcome it? We help our children face what they fear, not run from it. We understand that if we simply run from what we fear, we will always be controlled by that fear. This is why fathers teach their sons to stand up to the bully and face fear itself. We do this not because of the one bullying, but because fear will paralyze a life so that it cannot find relief. Consider so many verses through scripture:

> **Do not fear those who kill the body but are unable to kill the soul; but rather fear Him who is able to destroy both soul and body in hell.**
> **—Matthew 10:28**

Some consider this verse more threat than comfort. To understand it we need to revisit Daniel 3. As we talked about the "Fire" in the last chapter, I made it out to be the face of the enemy. It is also the door we must pass through or the challenge that must be overcome. Watch Shadrach, Meshach, and Abednego as they are marched to the fiery furnace. There is no other story in scripture that pushes this far into the threat, and yet God delivers them from harm. In other accounts, God stops the threat earlier or doesn't stop it at all.

So why did He wait so long? God could have stopped the scene when Nebuchadnezzar asked, "What God can deliver you from my hand?" God could have disintegrated his hand as He entered the room and addressed the question with, "I AM." As the soldiers went to heat the furnace, an armed force of fiery angels could have descended upon the kingdom.

There are so many moments in scripture when God caught the hand of Abraham as the knife was drawn, crumbled Goliath with a stone, and struck the enemies with leprosy, but here He doesn't. In this account, God doesn't stop the people or events that unfold. These individuals were just pawns on the chessboard. In this account God isn't worried about giants or kings; He goes after the real threat, death itself. The fire was the real enemy. The threat of burning alive was the point everyone watching the scene unfold feared—everyone, that is, except Shadrach, Meshach, and Abednego. These men had already stated it perfectly: "Our God, if he chooses to deliver us will, but even if He doesn't … we won't bow." Let me rephrase it just a little so you see my point: "But even if He doesn't … we won't break." These three men understood what scripture is telling us in Matthew. Take a moment to read the whole passage, and you will understand that God is trying to show us how to become *Untouchable*!

> A disciple is not above his teacher, nor a slave above his master. It is enough for the disciple that he become like his teacher, and the slave like his master. If they have called the head of the house Beelzebub, how much more will they malign the members of his household! Therefore do not fear them, for there is nothing concealed that will not be revealed, or hidden that will not be known. What I tell you in the darkness, speak in the light; and what you hear whispered in your ear, proclaim upon the housetops. Do not fear those who kill the body but are unable to kill the soul; but rather fear Him who is able to destroy both soul and body in hell.
>
> —Matthew 10:24–28

God chose to let them be thrown in and then allowed the men to walk around unharmed. Look at King Nebuchadnezzar now. What do you say to men whom the fire cannot touch? Basically the king says, "Okay, guys. You can come out now …" What else can he say? The scene is almost comical. He has nothing, and he knows it. What happens to a person once this veil is lifted? What happens when nothing of this world scares us anymore? So often, God answers our prayers by leading us to the thing we fear so we can face it. And in doing so we become untouchable in a sense. When this happens, it changes our perspectives, adjusts our wills to bend to His, and deepens our prayers.

"Lord, help me with this situation I'm in! *Not by taking it away but by providing Your strength so I may endure and outlast it.*"

"Lord, watch over my family and keep them safe, *and when trials come, give me strength to be the parent or spouse I need to be.*"

"Lord, take away the temptations that ensnare me, *by changing my mind, heart, and desires to be more like Yours. Lord, help me remember its intent to drag me from Your presence.*"

"Lord, I ask You to deliver me from this pain, *but until then, Lord, give me comfort during this trial.*"

"Father, humble those who have set themselves against me and broken my will to stand. *But if these things are Your will, Father, carry me because I don't have the ability to stand at the moment.*"

I believe these are the prayers God longs to hear. He strengthens, and we push forward in faith. By doing this we stop fearing the fire. Instead we push it open as a door to something more.

Am I saying we will come through it like Shadrach, Meshach, and Abednego? Yes, but not exactly. Sometimes death isn't stopped and physical pains will come. I'm saying you will find yourself at the point where the world can't touch you (your soul), and you find a deeper security in the hands of God.

Our words turn from prayers of wants to prayers of surrender. This is where the mother, praying for the health of her child, becomes a prayer for strength to help her family cope with what will be. This is where the man stops praying for God to punish the intoxicated driver who took the life of his wife and starts praying for strength and wisdom to help his children grow closer to God. These are the prayers that are examined by the world and are recognized by even the most bitter atheist. He may only jeer at the scene, but he takes notice and it challenges everything his logical mind has offered.

This is why God allows bad things to happen to good people. This is why we are not permitted to avoid pain and suffering. God has made us a *light to the world*, a light that is holy and set apart. How would the people of this world recognize Christians if all Christians were immune to suffering? If being a Christian meant you just had some light issues, but never anything serious, how would it affect the church? First, we would become idle as David did and fall face-first into sin. Second, the rest of the world would follow Him only for what they could gain. Life is about growing to become more like Him. When a true Christian endures pain, the world observes something that challenges every lie Satan has dared to tell. Consider how fast Satan must turn his grip loose in times of disaster and suffering when a nation is humbled. This is a scary thought for me, as I see a new angle from God's point of view. Sometimes those He has lifted up and blessed must suffer. It's Job's story, and sometimes we must play a part in it.

It's the subject of our prayers that God doesn't want us to hide from; "Lord, protect me from the world and the evil in it." We often don't connect pain and suffering with being a light to the world. The most effective lights in history have been the lives of those who have bled, suffered, and died for what they believe. What would the Bible have to offer us as means of encouragement if no one within its pages ever suffered? To be a light, to be holy, and to be set apart isn't a divine security plan for pain. Instead it is our call as Christians to simply live life by the same rules as everyone else, so that they can observe the differences between worldly comforts and godly ones— the difference between what God calls *untouchable* and what the world claims it to be. As Daniel chapter 3 begins, only three men fear

God and not the fire. At the end of the chapter, the entire kingdom can see God past the flames.

> **The fear of the LORD is the beginning of wisdom, And the knowledge of the Holy One is understanding.**
> **—Proverbs 9:10**

Do you see the depth of this verse?! This is the doorway (fear God, not the world) that makes us untouchable. And as understanding is given, we began to view things differently. Faith changes our perceptions.

Now, don't misunderstand me as I'm making this point. In no way am I suggesting we shouldn't pray for our families or loved ones while they hurt. Offering up prayers to our Father is an amazing blessing and comfort. I believe wholeheartedly in prayer and the power of God to move. But I understand that He sees a much bigger picture. We must trust Him to do what is best. In many cases the suffering and death of a Christian moves others. We don't know all the details, and we must surrender to His will. These prayers are the ones that help us accept it.

Prayer of Surrender

Lord, I have prayed relentlessly for Your help in this ordeal. I have pushed, promised, and pleaded that this storm would end so that I could stand once again in your presence rejoicing with family and friends thanking You. But I am terrified that answers I'm looking for will not come. I'm not doubting that You could fix everything right now if You wanted. And I still pray that you do exactly that. Yet I realize that some storms will not be lifted. I know that once You heard Your own Son plead with You for another outcome, and You couldn't grant His request without giving me up. If this path must be endured, please give me the comfort You gave Him. If I can't stand in Your presence to rejoice, hold me in Your arms as I experience what must be worse than death. I'm not asking for Your strength to fight; I'm just praying that the world doesn't break my faith in You.

'Pressing Forward in Stillness'

For to me, to live is Christ and to die is gain.
But if I am to live on in the flesh, this will
mean fruitful labor for me; and I do not know
which to choose.

—Philippians 1:21–22

Idleness is the Dead Sea that swallows all
virtues.

—Benjamin Franklin

Wasted away again in Margaritaville, searchin'
for my lost shaker of salt …

—Jimmy Buffet

Chapter 12

After the Fire

Is there a happily ever after on this side of the grave? So many people long for rest in this life and wonder when it will come. Paul asked his version of this question below:

> Because of the surpassing greatness of the revelations, for this reason, to keep me from exalting myself, there was given me a thorn in the flesh, a messenger of Satan to torment me—to keep me from exalting myself! Concerning this I implored the Lord three times that it might leave me.
>
> —II Corinthians 12:7–8

Paul has endured so much and asks repetitively that God removes this fire that torments him. He refers to it as his "thorn in the flesh." I love the way he centers the focus of his thorn around his flesh. He recognizes that the trials that tear him down physically don't necessarily cause him any harm spiritually. He goes on to accept this physical storm that God refuses to remove. He embraces it, understanding that the same physical tormentor is molding the spirit into something more Christlike.

Every year I watch as young men and women return to Gulf

Coast Bible Camp, each one a bit older and wiser. Every year I watch them come forward with "storms" in their lives, looking for a refuge. We are taught to come to God and cast our cares and troubles upon Him. So why do we find God handing those burdens right back to Paul in II Corinthians 12:9, 10? These two ideas of our "casting our burdens (or thorns) on Him" and "God allowing that thorn to come back as a tormentor to sharpen us" are quoted by many, but rarely together. They collide in the midst of trials. We try to balance our *longing for relief* while maintaining faith that *God has a purpose for not relieving us*. Perhaps we, like Paul, understand completely that trials will come. What we want to know is when they will end! And so the youth come and ask for prayers, hoping for God to remove the burdens.

They come forward hoping to rid themselves of the struggle. Many of us flock to Christ initially to find comfort, peace, and that sanctuary we all desire. And God gives us that; please understand this last point. God gives us peace and frees us from the chains of sin, but that is only the beginning. He then begins to mold us to be lights to the world. We connect to Him and begin to grow. Once we have matured past this early faith stage and anchored ourselves firmly in Him, He "sends us into all the world," which puts us back in the storms. We need to understand that Satan will always come after us and God will always strengthen us. It is an endless struggle with the physical body and the spiritual mind/heart. They sharpen one another. You can sit for a thousand years and contemplate this union of body and soul that God has created. They are like oil and water refusing to mix, and yet God has mixed them. He has done this for the purpose of growth (Romans 7:14–25).

This lesson is hard to understand for younger Christians, and it may feel like too much information for a teen. Many younger Christians are just starting that walk with God. They are in that wonderful and exciting stage of early faith, seeking and finding a God that is opening doors or calling them out on the water. They've not had time yet to see these trials. They fall in love with the passions and thrills of new life and assume they can skip the process of growing deeper into Christ. Later when trials come, they don't understand why the Utopia has vanished and simply struggle with what life has dealt them. They look for rest and comfort again, but the trials continue and so they leave the church looking for a new Utopia. If you have asked these questions of why God doesn't continue allowing us to live in a struggle-free environment, then once again God has answered my prayers of bringing this book to you. Now let's look into the scriptures and consider how the Spirit has shared thoughts on this.

We looked into the life of David earlier in this study. He must be the most-favored character in the Old Testament, the "man after God's own heart." Have you ever considered the sins of David as far as timing? Yes, we are very familiar with the act of adultery with Bathsheba and the murder of her husband, Uriah. Those who have studied him in depth will note his pride in numbering the nation later on in life and touch on parenting failures as well. I want to bring your attention to the timeline of David's failures. II Samuel 11:1 has been used to show David's idleness, and this is a valid point. When the time came for the king to go forth into battle, he became idle. He is still at war, but he isn't feeling the storms as he once did. There isn't much at stake. God has given him constant victory, so David simply leaves the fighting to someone else and doesn't enter the battlefield. He may have thought to himself, *The battle is the Lord's, after all.* I see a turning point in David's life here. His storms have faded. This is a David in earthly comfort. This is a different David.

As a youth he was isolated as the youngest in the fields and was sent a lion and a bear as he watched over the flocks (I Samuel 17:36). As David left this scene, he found another trial in front of Goliath. Goliath was defeated, and David became the son-in-law of Saul. But don't think this was peaceful. He was immediately assigned to the armies of Saul, where God continued to strengthen him in the fires of battle. As David grew more successful, Saul got jealous, and before David's ego could outgrow his head, Saul threw a javelin at it. For years David would run from the king, hiding in the countryside, caves, and even among the enemies of Israel. Even after Saul's death, things were difficult as David's transition to the throne unfolded. But what came "after the fires"?

Watch what happens when David finds a worldly peace. He is no longer on the battlefield against Goliath, nor is he being pursued by Saul and living on the run. Gone are the fires that once engulfed him, and he has arrived at the palace. Once he arrives in that place of comfort that we all long for, he is no longer the same person. When storms and fires are no longer present, what happens to the man after God's own heart? He loses focus on God and begins to entertain thoughts from the body. We have no mention of any wrong done by David before II Samuel 11. I'm sure he wasn't sinless, but yet while storms raged against him, scripture mentions nothing as far as faults go. That timeless description, "a man after God's own heart," was given to a young David (I Samuel 13:14).

After II Samuel 11:1, David falls into one temptation after another. Now compare King David to Uriah. Uriah has just come from the "fires" of the battlefield. Notice his mind-set and morals. He refuses to even sleep in his own home, much less with his wife. His reasoning? The armies of God still slept on the battlefield; why should he be resting in comfort? The trials of battle have made Uriah sharper. His passions for God and Israel are at a peak. In hindsight, I wonder if David caught a glimpse of his younger self in Uriah. I wonder if he remembered refusing the protection of Saul's armor, completely satisfied with only his passion for the Lord to clothe him as he charged Goliath. I doubt he did in that moment, but later he does list Uriah as one of his "mighty men" (II Samuel 23).

We see the same pattern again in David's situation in I Chronicles 21. The previous chapter ends with the death of the giants of Gath, and we find King David completing another trial or fire. With nothing going on in chapter 21, David decides to number the people. Regardless of the details of why this was sinful, we do know it was a pride thing that David enforced knowing it wasn't pleasing to God.

Search the scriptures, and see how many times sin was indulged in by believers when they were under attack or in dire need of refuge. We find Jonah living the good life and being called to service. He runs away. We find him in the belly of the great fish, now on his proverbial knees. He isn't considering anything ungodly when everything is crashing down around him.

Now consider how often believers chase after the world when they are at rest. From the very start at Eden it began, and through the centuries Israel continued to forget God's agenda once He gave them peace. Only in times of trials do we step up to the challenges, turn to God, and grow spiritually more mature.

So we come back to the question "What comes next after the fire'?" Is there a point where God will give us a Utopia on this side of the grave? The wisest man in all of scripture was given exactly that. King Solomon reached what all young men dream of: a sharp mind, health, power, riches, and respect. The Bible speaks of his wisdom and how great God made him in the sight of man, but I don't see his name referenced in Hebrews 11 and other passages that talk about spiritual giants. That's because he wasn't. The wisest man of all time was torn between God and worldliness later in life. Utopias weaken everything about our spiritual will!

So am I saying we don't need to rest? Of course not. I quoted some lyrics taken from Jimmy Buffet's well-known hit "Margaritaville" at the head of this chapter. I hope it got your attention. Don't get me wrong. I get a kick out of the song and many other country hits that have followed this theme. I turn the music up when I've had enough of life's demands. My body and mind desire an escape in response to everything the world has dealt me. I need relief!

Where do we go? The world says to take the music to heart. "Don't just blow some steam and listen to some beach music, make a 'Margarita' your sanctuary; indulge." We know this isn't the right plan. Our mind knows we should turn to God, and so we ask other Christians questions like, "How can I find peace?" or "What am I missing?" Something is wrong, and we can't quite put our finger on the answer.

Often we are told, "Get more involved in church; seeing the pain of others will put things in perspective for you!" Loved ones also advise, "Dig further into scripture to overcome the pain. You can beat it." Why do we advise others in times of despair to work harder? They suggest knowledge and understanding bring peace; yet sometimes I've had enough of that too and Solomon's words ring true.

> But beyond this, my son, be warned: the writing of many books is endless, and excessive devotion to books is wearying to the body.
> —Ecclesiastes 12:12

God understands when we need rest, and He provides it. God's peace is not given through events like Fat Tuesday during a Mardi Gras break. He hasn't given us permission to vacation from our roles as His children. He doesn't expect more work from us at these times either. Studying and gaining knowledge help prepare us for hard times, but that's not the comfort God provides when we have collapsed and are in need of the Great Physician. (I told you in chapter 7 we would come back to this thought.)

David found the answer. When he was pushed beyond his limits with trials, he submerged himself in God. He learned that God fills many different roles in our lives. He served the Great I AM, but when he had to rest he turned instead to the Good Shepherd. There is more to God than just duty, and when we need to rest we seek a different role that God plays. Instead of reaching the beach and heading to the bar, spend time on the shoreline and watch as the ocean waves renew the beach. Allow God to carry you as the timeless poem "Footprints in the Sand" so elegantly describes it. These things uplift the soul. It's standing in His presence once again, as you did when you first started your walk.

Learning to allow God to minister to you in this way can be difficult. We hear God's voice as he commands us to "seek and find" or "be still and know." These are commands that push us and help us grow. This is the voice concerned with our duties as Christians. The voice I am referring to now differs from that of duty. It is a call of comfort, and the message is similar: "Seek Me and find refuge" or "Be still and let Me love you."

The Gospel of John gives us a beautiful example of this notion, and we see how even Jesus's own apostles struggled with it.

> Then He poured water into the basin, and began to wash the disciples' feet and to wipe them with the towel with which He was girded. So He came to Simon Peter. He said to Him, "Lord, do You wash my feet?" Jesus answered and said to him, "What I do you do not realize now, but you will understand hereafter." Peter said to Him, "Never shall You wash my feet!" Jesus answered him, "If I do not wash you, you have no part with Me."
>
> —John 13:5–8

The key to this idea of feet washing is being still and allowing God to love you. This process can be taken further as the story continues to being still and allowing God to forgive you. Many people feel they don't deserve to be forgiven, and therefore "rest and comfort" are out of reach. Allowing God to love them, serve them, and minister to them in this way brings up the same emotions Peter struggled with: "*You will never touch my filth, Lord.*" How is it people forget He has already endured it?

It's children who find their parents in the stands as they perform on the sporting field. When they have a great game, they beam in their parents' direction. We love it when we've performed well, and we hope our parents have noticed. We want them to be proud us of. There is nothing wrong with wanting God to smile when He looks in your direction. If you don't, there is something wrong! However, on some days everything goes wrong and shame overcomes us. We don't look to the stands, because there is nothing to be proud of in our performance. Often we just want to be left alone. We don't want our parents or mentors to come and tell us it's okay, because we know we got creamed, embarrassed, and humiliated (Ref. 12:1).

It's the same emotion times a hundred as we struggle with the thorns and fires of this life. We wonder, *How can I face God with this? I don't want to bring my failures before Him.* The Father replies, *You are okay. You don't need to dwell on it.* We respond, *It's not okay! I failed and I'm in pain. I'll do better tomorrow. Tomorrow You'll see, and You will be proud.* Yet again we falter and struggle with the trials and thorns.

We want to overcome the pain these trials bring, so we try to push forward and throw some wins up on the scoreboard. We think some success will bring relief, but our strength leaves and getting up to fight another day just angers us. I don't want to be weak and in need; I want to stand strong enough to withstand anything. I want to become *untouchable* without having to run to Mommy and Daddy for comfort … And there it is. We want to stand on our own.

So now we come back full circle on our topic. Is there peace at the end of trials? What comes after the fire? The Father's comfort is given, and we are made ready for new storms. Paul understood that physical trials kept Him from exalting Himself from the desires to stand on his own. He had to accept that some fires would always come back, flare up. In those times he learned to collapse in the arms of God. This is the comfort and strength God gives. This process keeps us broken, and we must continue to allow God to wash us (I John 1:7). If we refuse His continuous cleansing grace, we give up the peace he provides within the flames. We forfeit the comfort He gives between the storms. And ultimately, we will lose the refuge He is beyond the grave.

Each of us is a light in some way, because we are all His workmanship. All of us have room to grow, and God desires that for us just as we desire it for our children. He refuses to let us remain idle, because therein lies the road to destruction. We understand spiritual life in the same way we understand the physical one. We are either growing or decaying. You can't simply stop the body and stall life, nor can you stop the spiritual life from growing or withering.

I would advise retreating from the world before entering this final prayer. Take some time to leave it behind. Music or a beautiful starry night could help. Wait until you feel what it's like to stand in awe of Him and then talk to Him.

> *My Father, my Savior and Comfort, please draw me
> into You and Your Spirit. Comfort me whether I'm in
> the fires or between them. Strengthen me for what's
> next, because only You know what lies before me.
> Help me not to be stressed about it but simply and
> purely enjoy Your presence for this moment. And
> once You've filled me up, I pray You help me share
> that presence with my family and even the world.*

And once He answers, please realize that because the world drains us we have to keep coming back to this place. We have to continue to turn our eyes back to take *A Second Look at the Savior: Hearing His Voice.*

'Pressing Forward in Stillness'

For we do not have a high priest who cannot sympathize with our weaknesses, but One who has been tempted in all things as we are, yet without sin.

—Hebrews 4:15

Chapter 13

The Ultimate Example

I had been studying with this lady for weeks. We hadn't talked about anything too personal, just some encouraging lessons and general stories in the Gospels. I believe she saw me as an opportunity perhaps ... maybe some help in paying bills, maybe some cash for groceries. For some reason she humored this short, white preacher boy who obviously hadn't been alive long enough to learn much about real-life problems.

As time passed, she grew less protective of how she felt. Glimpses of pain would appear from time to time, but only for a moment. She wasn't ready to share. One day I visited her when life had simply pushed her too far. She wasn't in the mood for our light daily study. Instead she had a real question that could not simply go unanswered. And so I found myself in her home, listening to her story.

She laid it all out: a heartbreaking tale that involved children she couldn't see, a man who only used her, a government that had trapped her, and a God who didn't answer. As she concluded her story, she fired her question at me: *"Where is God?"* Her question echoed a lifetime full of hurt behind it. *"Does He understand the way I feel? Does He know how heartbreaking it is to not be heard and left with this mess I call my life? Why doesn't He do something?"*

It was like she let me have both barrels, and the thing was she wasn't trying to hurt me with her question; she was truly wanting an answer. I was going over all she had said and searching my mind for a place to start. I had often used the advice an older minister had given to me when we were making hospital visits. He said, "Sometimes you need to keep your mouth shut and just cry with people. Sometimes there isn't an answer, or at least not the time to give one." I was so blown away by her pain that it took me a moment to process everything she was asking.

Many may read this book and be encouraged by the content. Others may become angry with this process and point back at God saying, "You don't understands how it feels to wait in silence." Are you sure He doesn't? Look again at our opening verse in Hebrews 4:15. I listed only one on this chapter because I don't want any distraction here. God claims to understand every way in which we feel tempted. That includes how Satan twists questions, silence, and fires that are presented in life. If you have to ask the question "Do you understand, Lord?" by all means ask it. But do so without pride, and in humbleness listen to the answers provided in scripture.

Take the time now to talk to Him in prayer. Tell Him your frustration, but do it respectfully. Once you've asked, put all distraction away as we begin it again. All chapters of this book will be touched on as they are introduced in bold text.

1-The Question; -The Beginning

> In the beginning God created the heavens and the earth. The earth was formless and void, and darkness was over the surface of the deep, and the Spirit of God was moving over the surface of the waters. Then God said, "Let there be light"; and there was light.
>
> —Gen 1:1-3

As we continue reading Genesis, we come to these statements.

> Then God said, "Let the waters below the heavens be gathered into one place, and let the dry land appear"; and it was so. God called the dry land earth, and the gathering of the waters He called seas; and God saw that it was good.
>
> —Genesis 1:9–10

Notice what takes place in this verse. God forms all the dry lands of the earth. Mountain ranges and valleys are formed. From the wild jungles to the beautiful coastlines that outline the continents, God shaped them all. At some point in this day God even designs a plot of land that had to make Him pause and consider everything ... a simple area that may change over the years to come through the flood and other natural disasters. Still this place had to be designed. A place that eventually would be called Golgotha. This fact blows my mind. God created the land area that would one day host the crucifixion of His Son, and yet at the end of the day He looked over it and "saw that it was good." The question that we ask was a question God Himself considered as He started this whole thing. Who is God? God's version of the question would have been, "Who AM I?" And from the very beginning, He answers the question that would become clearer to us over the next four thousand years. He is the everlasting Father, the very definition of love, grace and truth combined (I John 4:8; John 1:14).

As He designed the world, He designed His role in our lives. He has been true to that role ever since. Two thousand years ago God sent His Son into the world. And His name shall be Immanuel, which translates to "God with us." This name tells us who He is and why He came. This brings us to our next point.

2-Seeking Answers; The Birth

> And the Word became flesh, and dwelt among us, and
> we saw His glory, glory as of the only begotten from the
> Father, full of grace and truth.
>
> —John 1:14

God becomes a man and dwells among us. He came seeking to give answers. According to Matthew 7:7, everyone who seeks will find. Find what, though? That's the real question. Consider this verse.

> These things I have written to you who believe in the
> name of the Son of God, so that you may know that you
> have eternal life.
>
> —I John 5:13

Notice the answers He provides are written down in His everlasting Word. He never intended for me to look to my heart for security. My feelings are up and down from day to day. Looking to how I feel for security and answers would put me on an emotional roller coaster. Despite this, many still place their anchors upon themselves. They are souls tossed about on the waves of uncertainty in life. He came to provide rock-solid answers, and more so He came to show us God.

3-What Do You Want from Me? His Ministry

> So Jesus answered them and said, "My teaching is
> not Mine, but His who sent Me. If anyone is willing
> to do His will, he will know of the teaching, whether
> it is of God or whether I speak from Myself. He who
> speaks from himself seeks his own glory; but He who is
> seeking the glory of the One who sent Him, He is true,
> and there is no unrighteousness in Him."
>
> —John 7:16–18

Jesus came to do the Father's will. While He ministered here on earth, He constantly asked that God's will be done in His life. He didn't have to ask what God wanted, because they were One. This doesn't mean that Christ never thought about the options the world offered. He was tempted just as we are, yet Jesus refrained because He chose to mirror God's will, making the Father's plan one with His own. He reminds the apostles of this right before He is betrayed. Notice the request of Philip.

> Philip said to Him, "Lord, show us the Father, and it is enough for us." Jesus said to him, "Have I been so long with you, and yet you have not come to know Me, Philip? He who has seen Me has seen the Father; how can you say, 'Show us the Father'? Do you not believe that I am in the Father, and the Father is in Me? The words that I say to you I do not speak on My own initiative, but the Father abiding in Me does His works."
>
> —John 14: 8–10

Philip is seeking answers from God. Even more so he desires to see God. Christ's response is simple. He came to show us the Father. They are one and the same. And when we examine Christ, we see the Father and the Spirit as well. He allows us to look at wonders and mysteries that even the angels longed to understand (I Peter 1:12). A visual example has been given in Christ's time spent with us. Jesus now asks from us the same command that He received from His Father, "Abide in Me!" He understands!

4-What's Stopping You? Entering Jerusalem

Does God understand how it feels when we are called to push forward when we prefer an alternate route? Does He understand the things that stop us from following? Has He felt fears that paralyze both mind and body to the point neither seems to respond? Has He experienced the pain of betrayal by loved ones and the sting of having to face them or, worse yet, forgive them? Does God know the chilling call of the grave and the pain we must suffer first before taking death's hand?

> Now before the Feast of the Passover, Jesus knowing that His hour had come that He would depart out of this world to the Father, having loved His own who were in the world, He loved them to the end. During supper, the devil having already put into the heart of Judas Iscariot, the son of Simon, to betray Him, Jesus, knowing that the Father had given all things into His hands, and that He had come forth from God and was going back to God, got up from supper, and laid aside His garments; and taking a towel, He girded Himself.
>
> —John 13:1–4

He knows all of these feelings that challenge us. All of the different fiery darts that Satan hurls in our direction have caused Him the same pain. As He enters Jerusalem, so many "fiery furnaces" are being cranked up before Him, but nothing stops Christ. Why? Consider the verses above (John 13:1–4) again as they set the scene. Christ knew who God was, and He knew who He Himself was. He understood the Father's will and accepted it. These are the exact truths that we must cling to in order to become *unstoppable*. He understands!

5-Here … You Try -The Upper Room through Gethsemane

> Then He poured water into the basin, and began to wash the disciples' feet and to wipe them with the towel with which He was girded.
>
> —John 13:5

God has also played the part He asks us to carry out. We are servants. Do You understand the place of a slave, Lord? Would You like to try to accomplish the impossible, only to realize you need help from the one who put the task before you?

> **Have this attitude in yourselves which was also in Christ Jesus, who, although He existed in the form of God, did not regard equality with God a thing to be grasped, but emptied Himself, taking the form of a bond-servant, and being made in the likeness of men. Being found in appearance as a man, He humbled Himself by becoming obedient to the point of death, even death on a cross.**
>
> **—Philippians 2:5–8**

Countless emotions play out in this scene of Jesus from the upper room to Gethsemane. A storm larger than we could ever imagine is about to engulf Him. His heart has been stolen. "Lord, please take this cup from me!" His strength is spent. He has ministered to His apostles nonstop from the upper room to Gethsemane. Jesus seeks to find a door of escape, but none is given. He asks the Father to take the storm away, but God does not. The response? Be still, my Son, and know. Does God understand how we feel when more is asked of us than we could possibly give? He understands! And in those moments when Christ pours all of His strength out for His followers, and still God requires more from Him, He turns to God for strength in prayer.

6-Where Will You Meet the Stone? The Garden

Remember the lady I began to tell you about at the beginning of the chapter. Allow me to finish that story now. As I looked back to her, I noticed a painting above her head. It had been there every time I had visited. It was a well-known painting that most of you have seen and many of you may own. It was a scene out of scripture from over two thousand years ago that now cried out to me as I had never heard it before. It was the picture of Christ in the garden of Gethsemane just before Judas enters. He is kneeling in prayer over a stone, looking to His Father in tears. I brought her attention to this painting, and now I bring it to yours.

Does Christ understand what it means to "meet the stone"? To accept what God has asked and bend to His will? This is where everything changes and the path Jesus now faces points toward the cross. Here in the garden, Christ chooses to fall upon the stone and become broken; there is no turning back. He understands how it feels to *break* upon the stone!

> **But those that wait upon the Lord will receive new strength. They will fly as high as eagles. They will run and not get tired. They will walk and not grow weak.**
> **—Isaiah 40:31**

The storm was not taken away, but Jesus was lifted up on wings like an eagle, empowered to fly over this storm and conquer it. In prayer He finds strength, and God sends angels to minister to Him. In a moment He will leave this place and the silence will begin ...

7-The Silence; Mock Trial

In just a moment His own follower, Judas, will stand before Him. A friend whom Jesus has taught and traveled with over the last three years will kiss His cheek in betrayal. How do you stand in this moment, much less all that is to follow? In only minutes all of His followers will scatter from Him. Most He will not see again until after the grave. Within an hour He will stand before His enemies in a mock trial that is illegal in itself. Witnesses will be called to testify against Him. Only silence will speak on His behalf. The self-righteous religious leaders of the day will call forth witness after witness to twist the truth, and no one will speak on behalf of Christ. Through all of this Jesus will hear silence from the heavens. Considering this, I have to admire his actions.

> Now the chief priests and the whole Council kept trying to obtain false testimony against Jesus, so that they might put Him to death. They did not find any, even though many false witnesses came forward. But later on two came forward, and said, "This man stated, 'I am able to destroy the temple of God and to rebuild it in three days.'" The high priest stood up and said to Him, "Do You not answer? What is it that these men are testifying against You?" But Jesus kept silent. And the high priest said to Him, "I adjure You by the living God, that You tell us whether You are the Christ, the Son of God." Jesus said to him, "You have said it yourself; nevertheless I tell you, hereafter you will see THE SON OF MAN SITTING AT THE RIGHT HAND OF POWER, and COMING ON THE CLOUDS OF HEAVEN."
>
> —Matthew 26:59–64

This passage shows how Christ simply mirrored His Father and stood in silence as they did their best to condemn Him. Finally, the high priest, frustrated at their feeble attempts to trap Christ in trickery, just asked Him, "Are You God?" Jesus finally responds to a straightforward question with a straightforward answer. He gives them the angle they were looking for and prepares to stand still and know that God is!

8-Be Still -Before Pilate

> Therefore Pilate said to Him, "So You are a king?" Jesus
> answered, "You say correctly that I am a king. For this I
> have been born, and for this I have come into the world,
> to testify to the truth. Everyone who is of the truth
> hears My voice." Pilate said to Him, "What is truth?"
> —John 18:37–38

As Christ talks with Pilate, He states, " For this I have been born,
and for this I have come into the world, to testify to the truth." He
recognizes that His entire life and existence have been in preparation
to testify to the truth even as a man prepares to sit in the judgment
seat and put God on trial.

Everything that the Jews and Romans are putting on Him
makes a mockery of God. In the same instance everything being
carried out prepares Christ to become the sacrificial Lamb. Jesus
understands the events—every small, painful detail—as submission
to God's time and will. Does He know what it feels like to be on
God's anvil? To be molded and modeled by the Divine Blacksmith?
He understands!

9-And Know that I AM God; Through the Scourging

Jesus hears the rejection of His people. About one million Jews
cry out, "Crucify Him, let His blood be on us and our children."
Oh, how cruel irony can be! These are the same Jews who just
praised His coming a few days ago. The mocking of the soldiers,
the crown of thorns, and a purple robe were all designed to destroy
His very spirit. These things brought mental pain that matched the
physical pain He would soon endure. The scourging, this process
alone, would have caused most to seek an alternative route, another
source of peace beside God's will. Please understand that angels are

still His to command. Can you imagine what Jesus could see? Ten thousand angels on the edge of destroying everything with their eyes fixed on their Lord. To truly understand how Jesus endured this path, we must understand that His finger is on the "eject" button. Humanity pushes Him beyond what is humanly possible. Yet He endures.

Have you ever considered this? As Jesus is about to be nailed to the cross, He cries out to the Father, "Forgive them, they do not know what they are doing!" Could Christ have been trying to comfort the Father, knowing that God wanted to act? If so we have a picture of Christ telling the Father to *be still*. We always recognize the pain and suffering of the Son, but what would hurt more—being crucified, or watching your child be crucified unjustly while having the power to stop it at any given moment? The Father is about to be separated from the Son by our sins. Jesus is not the only Godhead that must endure pain and suffering. Please realize, they are both *still* as they endure the crucifixion process. And both stay true to the course of action, because they both "*know* God's plan and God's will." They understand!

10-The Fire; The Crucifixion

Christ has been brought to Golgotha, a place He, the Father, and the Holy Spirit designed so long before. I wonder whether or not He recalls the end of that third day when they looked over this area and in agreement said, "It is good." Now, forty centuries later, the crucifixion is upon Him. The Son will be separated from the Father. The sins of all humanity will be laid upon Him. His destination is clear: nails driven into His hands and feet, parched with thirst, and stripped of His clothing for the entire world to see His shame. His mother's eyes are full of questions as all of these events unfold before her.

Why do it? Why allow Yourself to be thrown into the fire? Why remain there six hours upon the cross? I understand the theological reasoning behind this event: "We needed a perfect sacrifice." Yet that doesn't do it justice! He could have simply sent an angel to die in His place. He could have chosen to die a quicker death or at least chosen to feel less pain. There are a thousand different ways He could have justified any of these directions, and preachers could still put a great spin on it.

The questions don't stop there. Why experience any of the last thirty-three years? He could have simply come onto the scene as a prophet would have in the Old Testament. He could have entered Jerusalem, offended everyone with the truth, and been killed for speaking on God's behalf. The whole thing would have taken less than a week. Why approach this in the longest, most painful, drawn-out way imaginable?

I believe the answer lies in this question. *"What more could He have given?"* The Father gives up the Son. He made His dwelling place among us for about thirty-three years. He knows what worldly "fires" are. In the end, if we accept the Bible as truth, you can't argue that God doesn't care. You can't claim He doesn't understand how you feel.

11- Untouchable; The Whole Experience

There are evils in this world that I've not touched on in this book. Fires that shake me to my core. People born with diseases for which there are no cures. Children abducted and sold in sex trafficking circles. Meaningless killings of saints or sinners. I am not oblivious to these extreme situations. And when we must endure them, when we are thrown into the most intense storms that life can produce and find only God's silence, this one point remains. What more could He have given to you to show He cares and understands? He lived, suffered, and died so that this point is "untouchable." This one point separates Christianity from all man-made religions.

He lived through all of it. Even more so, He has done it for those who may currently be the cause of your grief. For the world He died. And for those who waste that gift and cause others only pain, they will meet a vengeful judge in the end. He knows too well what awaits them, and if they were my children, I would beg God to grant them just a little more time to repent.

If you are in the fires of this life, look to our Comforter. The Holy Spirit's greatest work is the Bible.

Consider the story of Joseph, a young man betrayed and sold into slavery. God is with Him. For years in silence he endures and is molded to do great things for God. His father, Jacob, suffers and endures so much pain at losing his son. God is silent on the truth of the situation but understands and comforts him still.

Consider the story of Shadrach in chapter 10. While reading the story afresh, were you excited? Why? It is, however, a story of young men being abducted by a foreign enemy. Can you imagine the prayers lifted to God on behalf of the parents or relatives of these children? Heartbreaking questions and requests that were answered only by God's silence at that time? We don't think of this story in those terms, though. Would you like to know why we don't see it as a story of abduction? It's because we know the ending. Knowing the whole story makes it a story of encouragement and great faith. In this way we catch a glimpse of how God sees all stories, because He knows the endings.

God doesn't expect us not to hurt or be angry. I believe we are allowed to throw all of those emotions at Him just like Job did. Questioning but trusting. In all that pain Job never spoke evil of God. Faith can make one untouchable.

12-After the Fire; Snapshots of Christ in Prayer

> I have fought the good fight, I have finished the course,
> I have kept the faith; in the future there is laid up for
> me the crown of righteousness, which the Lord, the
> righteous Judge, will award to me on that day; and
> not only to me, but also to all who have loved His
> appearing.
>
> —II Tim 4:7,8

Christ simply went from one set of problems to the next. Never did he find an earthly peace. And when His strength was spent, He didn't study more or work harder. He simply found moments of heavenly peace in prayer before His Father between the fires. He didn't report in to the Lord and Commander for orders. Instead, He sought out "Jehovah Rohi" (The Lord My Shepherd) and let the Father minister to Him. If God needed God's comfort, how much more should we seek it?!

We were never meant to arrive in this life at complete rest. It's the next life where God promises us this final refuge. People refer to this life as a test, a struggle, and a race. I would suggest to you that life, in its purest definition, is to grow. We gain wisdom through pain and laughter, during heartaches and times of rejoicing. God has designed us as children, and so growth is implied.

We get one life. What will you do with yours? We can't control the time or circumstances, but we can choose to grow closer to Him.

Prayer Request

I hope this study has helped you on your journey in life and with struggles you face. I hope God has opened your eyes and ears a little wider, as He has opened mine. At this point I wonder what will happen to this book. Do I push or remain still? Whatever the case,

I ask a favor from you. Please keep my family and this effort in your prayers. Other books sit outlined on this computer, and my prayer is that if God wants them finished, a door will open. Or perhaps, because we serve such a creative God, He will just shove me out a window. :)

Closing Thoughts

For God so loved the world, that He gave His only begotten Son, that whoever believes in Him shall not perish, but have eternal life.
—John 3:16

Now why do you delay? Get up and be baptized, and wash away your sins, calling on His name.
—Acts 22:16

And the testimony is this, that God has given us eternal life, and this life is in His Son. He who has the Son has the life; he who does not have the Son of God does not have the life. These things I have written to you who believe in the name of the Son of God, so that you may know that you have eternal life.
—I John 5:11–13

Chapter 14

Hearing His Call, in Faith

As we close this study on hearing God's voice and understanding how to apply that voice in life, I find myself compelled to share this study on God's call to us. Salvation has been presented in so many directions today it's frustrating to get a biblical answer. Like for most topics, many overcomplicate or oversimplify God's plan to redeem us. I believe too many times we approach the scriptures with preconceived notions on what is involved with becoming a Christian, because if there is one thing we are sure about, it's that we are saved. All those arts and crafts I worked on as a child in Sunday school attest to this.

Do me a favor. Ask a church if they understand every doctrine perfectly and see how they respond. "Well, no, we don't have a perfect understanding of everything." Now simply run down every doctrine taught by that church and ask if that's the one they don't grasp perfectly. It's funny when you itemize the list how the answers change to, "Oh, that one we understand and teach perfectly." Let down your defense for a moment and just search the scriptures with me. You have nothing to lose and only another's insight to gain. I hope to show you how scriptures coexist, and how often we see only what we concentrate on.

Let me start with this. If you begin our conversation with, "How are you saved?" my response is now and will always be, "Jesus Christ on the cross!" That was the act that saved me, and it wasn't free. Jesus paid dearly for it. I know what people mean when they say, "Salvation is a free gift," but that can be so misleading. Romans chapter 5 refers to salvation as a free gift, meaning I can't "earn" salvation. That is an excellent truth that I embrace, because I could never earn God's grace. Yet to say salvation costs me nothing is wrong. Becoming a Christian involves making a covenant with God. I am giving Him my life! To say salvation costs me nothing is to say loving someone costs me nothing. My only point before we really dive into the topic is this. We need to stop cheapening God's gift of salvation to the point it has been compared to a man handing out a million dollars. And all I have to do is ask for it and enjoy blessings. Would you compare marriage, taking a wife, like this?

America has reinvented Christianity as something like a social club at a college. I join and experience college a few years. After I've been there, done that, I am considered an alumnus forever regardless of what I do. Christianity is a lifestyle, not just experiences and deeds that filled my teenage years. Becoming a Christian cost me everything I am.

In order to receive God's gift of salvation, we must have faith (I John 5:11–13). Everyone agrees on this point, but then most define "faith" as just "belief." Let's start here. What is the difference between these words? The Bible teaches us that even demons believe in God (James 2:19). Satan believes in God; how couldn't he when he has to present himself before God when called (Job 1:6)? Preachers of all backgrounds will follow me on this point. "Yes, the devil believes in God," but if I ask, "Do the demons have faith in God?" they pause for a moment a bit unsure. Therein lies my point. We know there is a difference. Now, some will continue with, "Yes, the devil has faith," because they use belief and faith interchangeably. That is a basic principle that many need to reexamine. People continue to think this way because we want to keep the gift simple and marketable to the world. "Just believe it ... so easy a child could do it."

Please turn over and read Hebrews chapter 11 again. This section of scripture has been nicknamed, "The Great Hall of Faith." Let's consider some of the highlights: verse 4, "By faith Able offered"; verse 7, "By faith Noah ...prepared"; verse 8, "By faith Abraham ... obeyed"; verse 17, "By faith Abraham ... offered"; verse 20, "By faith Isaac ... blessed"; and verse 24, "By faith Moses ... refused." And as the writer of Hebrews closes his thoughts on faith ...

> And what more shall I say? For time will fail me if I tell of Gideon, Barak, Samson, Jephthah, of David and Samuel and the prophets, who by faith conquered kingdoms, performed acts of righteousness, obtained promises, shut the mouths of lions, quenched the power of fire, escaped the edge of the sword, from weakness were made strong, became mighty in war, put foreign armies to flight. Women received back their dead by resurrection; and others were tortured, not accepting their release, so that they might obtain a better resurrection; and others experienced mockings and scourgings, yes, also chains and imprisonment. They were stoned, they were sawn in two, they were tempted, they were put to death with the sword; they went about in sheepskins, in goatskins, being destitute, afflicted, ill-treated (men of whom the world was not worthy), wandering in deserts and mountains and caves and holes in the ground.
>
> And all these, having gained approval through their faith ...
>
> —Hebrews 11:32–39

As we look over this chapter, we are told faith is more than simply believing in God. Faith is our belief in motion. To become a Christian is to make a covenant with God (Hebrews 7:22–25). Making a covenant always requires an action, even if it is simply stating "I do" at a wedding ceremony. To say nothing must be done would rewrite the definition of faith: "By faith Abraham, when called to go, believed God, but did nothing God asked him to do." That makes no sense whatsoever.

I remember hearing a wonderful illustration on the word *faith* as I was growing up. The story was probably an embellished account of Jean-François Gravelet's feats in the 1850s. The story was of a man who dared to walk a tightrope over Niagara Falls. The man asked the onlookers if they believed he could accomplish the feat. The responses were laughter and scolding for even considering it. "No?" the man echoed back to the crowd. He then walked the tightrope over the falls and then back again. The crowds cheered and in astonishment replied they now believed he could do it. After a moment the man asked the crowd if they believed he could push a wheelbarrow across the tightrope. Again the crowd laughed and shook their heads no. The man proceeded to push the wheelbarrow across the tightrope and back again. A cheer went up from the onlookers, even louder than before. Now they chanted, "We believe you can do it!" The man asked the crowds, "Do you think I could put a person in the wheelbarrow and cross the rope again?" The crowds continued their chant, "We believe you can do it!" At this point the man smiled at the people and asked for a volunteer. The chanting died out, and no one moved. This is the difference between simple "belief" and "faith." Faith moves, acts, speaks, dares, listens, and obeys. Faith would get in the wheelbarrow!

Consider the example of Moses. God tells Moses to stretch out his rod over the waters and then He will split the sea. Could Moses have had faith without lifting the rod? Imagine that conversation.

God: Moses, lift your rod over the sea, and I will divide the waters and deliver my people. As far as the Egyptians are concerned, I will destroy them all today.

Moses: "Lord, that sounds great. But the thing is, I'm really tired from fleeing Egypt and mentally exhausted from the ten plagues. I totally believe you can split this sea, so could we skip the theatrics and get on with it?"

Would God have honored Moses's request?

Again, take Joshua's story. God commands Joshua to march around Jericho for seven days. They are told to parade each day, playing their horns and making a spectacle of themselves. Joshua could have responded, "Lord, I know you are the one true God and that this city is yours to command. In my opinion it would be a waste of time spending all week whooping and yelling about all this. It sounds like a lot of work for nothing. I'm just going to tell the people to get ready for the walls to fall, and as soon as You drop them, I will lead the people in." Would God have crumbled the walls?

Argue all you like; the answer is simply, "No." Faith has always been demonstrated through our actions. It is "belief in motion." Someone wants to contest this reasoning with **Ephesians. 2:8- 9: "For by grace you have been saved through faith; and that not of yourselves, it is the gift of God; not as a result of works, so that no one may boast."** This is a beautiful passage that must be considered and balanced with the rest of scripture. How would this verse apply to what I am suggesting to you?

It would apply to Joshua if after the walls crumbled he stood before the people and said, "Look what our marching has accomplished! We have crumbled the walls." Only a fool would credit his "work" for what God had done as they stand in the walls' ruins! But this doesn't mean the work isn't necessary. Imagine Moses standing on the other side of the Red Sea giving himself praise for his amazing skills with a stick. This is folly, but it doesn't mean that the work didn't have to take place. Some may feel this teaching is too childish. Surely God wouldn't have all these scriptures making such an elementary point. Surely God knows that a true follower wouldn't have to be taught that the Lord alone performs the miracle and would never credit themselves and their stick. Follow Moses's story on to Numbers 20:10–11, and we find Moses claiming credit for God's miracle as he and his stick are at it again. God punishes Moses for his self-righteous act and doesn't allow him to go into the promised land.

We are under the New Covenant, which begins after the crucifixion. The Holy Spirit falls upon the apostles, and a new age begins. Peter kicks the whole thing off in Acts chapter 2. Those now living under this New Covenant respond to Peter's invitation.

> Now when they heard this, they were pierced to the heart, and said to Peter and the rest of the apostles, "Brethren, what shall we do?" Peter said to them, "Repent, and each of you be baptized in the name of Jesus Christ for the forgiveness of your sins; and you will receive the gift of the Holy Spirit. For the promise is for you and your children and for all who are far off, as many as the Lord our God will call to Himself."
> —Acts 2:37–39

Peter was given the "keys to the kingdom" in Matthew 16:17–19, and now he opens the doors. We are told exactly what baptism is:

> Or do you not know that all of us who have been baptized into Christ Jesus have been baptized into His death? Therefore we have been buried with Him through baptism into death, so that as Christ was raised from the dead through the glory of the Father, so we too might walk in newness of life.
> —Romans 6:3–4

It is a symbolic act where we bury the old man and God raises us up to walk a new life in Christ. By no means did the water save me; it was and will always be Christ. But that doesn't mean it's not necessary. Romans goes on to say,

> **But thanks be to God that though you were slaves of sin, you became obedient from the heart to that form of teaching to which you were committed.**
>
> **—Romans 6:17**

Notice the wording? "became obedient from the heart to that form of teaching." What form of teaching did they obey from the heart? I believe that must be what was covered in verses 3–16.

A wedding ceremony can be described with the same reasoning. Why would one argue that making a vow before witnesses isn't needed when one takes a wife? Why complain about a simple task God has required of us? It's as if people can't compute these verses, because of preconceived notions. Then they basically claim I am trying to give all the credit to the state of Tennessee for joining my wife and me and making us "one flesh." Or maybe the altar. That's absurd! God joins man and woman in marriage, but he has required us to have some form of commitment before witnesses. That may be a preacher and family, or that may be a courthouse clerk, but it has to take place. Why argue with that? Too many make the argument that Naaman made in II Kings chapter 5. *But it just doesn't make sense to me.*

Some will shake their heads and quote John 3:16. They return to the nutshell version of the quick and easy. Yet they fail to grasp that John 3:16 tells us the exact same thing. Jesus is concluding a conversation with Nicodemus.

> For God so loved the world, that He gave His only
> begotten Son, that whoever believes in Him shall not
> perish, but have eternal life.
>
> —John 3:16

Jesus closes that statement with "whoever believes in Him ..."
Jesus is speaking of himself in the third person. Believes what? In
Him, in everything He just finished telling Nicodemus he must do.
Go back and read what Jesus tells Nicodemus in verses 2–15.

Now, there is a reason most *smart* writers/authors stay away
from doctrinal issues. Keep in mind I've never been accused of being
a "smart writer." There are always more passages to consider and
explanations to make—Cornelius, the thief on the cross, and the
Corinthians, to name a few. I have written this information to seekers
of God's Word. I hope that you take it and add it to other information
you come across. Ultimately you are the one accountable to God,
and I hope you never stop searching the scriptures to understand
God and His will for your life.

So to recap these thoughts or to simply sum them up ... We are
saved by Christ through faith. Faith is our belief in motion. Under
the New Covenant we are told,

> Now why do you delay? Get up and be baptized, and
> wash away your sins, calling on His name.
>
> —Acts 22:16

> [W]ho once were disobedient, when the patience
> of God kept waiting in the days of Noah, during
> the construction of the ark, in which a few, that is,
> eight persons, were brought safely through the water.
> Corresponding to that, baptism now saves you—not
> the removal of dirt from the flesh, [*not the act*] but
> an appeal to God for a good conscience [*your belief*

in motion—faith] —**through the resurrection of Jesus Christ.** -(*Emphasis mine*)

—I Peter 3:20–21

We shouldn't try to dissect faith into different parts but simply accept it all as one. Will you hear His Word? I hope you have enjoyed this book, and I hope it has challenged you, because writing it has done both for me.

Prayer Request

As you continue your prayers to God, please keep me in them. As a fellow seeker of God, I have prayed for all those who read this book. I have prayed that despite my ability to word or describe these topics, that God will give you understanding from His Word. That's why I used so many scripture references. I'm sure they are correct! :)

Please pray for my wife, Jessica, and my children, Autumn and Caleb. Thank you so much.

—Byron Smith

Study Guide

A Second Look at the Savior: Hearing His Voice

I spent some time reworking these chapters into a class series. These guides will contain highlighted points to discuss in each chapter of the book. New illustrations and activities have been added for classroom participation. My hope is that the involvement produced through these activities will create an atmosphere of discovering lessons before you look at the scriptures. I have worked with young people now for over twenty years, and I've found that if visuals or activities can be used, they should be. In college one professor put it this way: "Tell them and they will forget, show them and they will remember, involve them and they will understand."

Introductions: As you begin teaching this book as a series, the introductions are very important. Your goal is to help them enter the mind-set of the topic before you discuss it. Opening any class this way will increase input from the students.

Please remember to take time here. With teaching, so often we rush into a lesson because it is familiar to us and we want to share it. This is like driving off to the restaurant with your wife clinging to an opened passenger door with one foot being drug across the pavement. Allow them to enter the mind-set before entering the lesson.

Study Guide: 1) The Question

Introduction:

Assign the class different roles. One will be a Buddhist, another a Muslim. You can mix up some other fun titles, like a hobbit who believes in Middle Earth theology or maybe someone from Asgard that acknowledges Thor as his or her god, *ensuring creative discussion afterward.* You will also want someone to represent Christianity. You can have the rest of the class fall into groups that your volunteers represent. Now ask the question, "Who is right?"

Of course everybody thinks they are right. Now ask how they know. Most of the time you will have a few use the words, "I know because I can feel it in my heart." You may even have the Christian representative use this reason. If you use Thor, search the web for "Iceland builds temple to Thor."

Point 1

> The heart is more deceitful than all else and is desperately sick; Who can understand it?
> —Jeremiah 17:9

Discussion: Why is the heart described as wicked, and if it is wicked, why would God want it?

We concluded that the heart is wicked when it replaces God's role in our lives. God never intended our heart to be our guide.

Point 2

Please visit my website asecondlookbook.com for an introduction video on universalism.

Point 3

Going back to the introduction, how many people use what they feel as a guide? Do we do the same? If so, how many people are actually just redesigning a god in their own image? If we decide what that god should stand for, we are at the heart of that god.

Term to discuss: Self-led self-righteousness

There is another phrase used often by believers: "I believe God is opening doors and I need to follow?" Is this the same feeling?

Our guide is different Psalms 119:105 and I John 5:13 because guidelines have been set to assure we can separate personal desires from the Spirit's calling.

Conclusion: What is the role of the Holy Spirit?

Is the Spirit of God like the human spirit? We describe our spirits as wild, free, and untamable. That sounds nice, and are excited by seeing ourselves as unpredictable. Often we confuse the Holy Spirit with the same mind set of unpredictable, but is this true?

In John chapter 16, we find that He is not pushing His own agenda, but instead magnifies the teachings of Christ. When the Spirit pulls on our hearts or we believe God is leading us to action, that guidance must line up with the Spirit's greatest work, the Bible. It must coincide with the teachings of Christ. The Spirit may surprise in the approach, but never strays from the guidelines set in scripture.

II Peter 1:20-21 and II Timothy 3:16–17

Study Guide: 2) Seeking Answers

Introduction: When Jesus Christ came, He was met with a vast ocean of questions. Imagine if Christ visited our class tonight. What questions would you like to ask Him? When we really dive into this question two thoughts rise to the top. "Who are You Lord?" "What do You want from me?"

Can anything good come out of Nazareth? This was Nathaniel's version of, "Who are You?" —John 1:46

The reply, "Come and see," is another form of "Seek and find."

Point 1. Is it wrong to ask questions?

Hebrews 11:1 teaches us, ""Faith is the substance of things hope for, and the *evidence of things unseen*" (emphasis mine). Faith is "evidence of things unseen" as well. "Proof of things hidden" is another way to phrase it. Please note 1 John 5:13

Matthew 14:22–33: In what ways did Peter see evidence?

He gave us His Word (Psalm 119:135), tells us to pursue Him (Matthew 6:33), and then tells us how (Matthew 7:7).

Point 2. The two questions (read both accounts)

> What do you say about him, since he opened your eyes?
> —Pharisees' Question, John 9:17

> Who are you, Lord?
> —Saul's Question, Acts 9:5

How are these questions similar? The same basic inquiry - same a Pharisees background and theology. However, are both questions sincere in the search.

What were the Jews looking for in Jesus?

What did they find?

When we ask the question, "Who are you, God," have we answered the question for Him?

We can't produce both sides of the conversation.

Point 3. What are some things that make it hard to hear God's voice clearly

Anger and pride got in the way of the Pharisees in Acts 9.

John 9:24. They had heard the answer once already, but it didn't make sense to them. Why? Because they just knew Jesus was a sinner. How?

Consider the chapter illustration of the square circle.

Now let's look at the conclusion of Saul's story in Acts 9

God actually takes away Saul's sight to help Him see.

If we don't allow God to answer in His own way and accept that answer, we allow bitterness to consume us, pull us away from Him, and ultimately destroy us.

Attitude changes the way we perceive answers. Refer to the example of the woman praying for food in the chapter.

Conclusion: John 9:39–40. Jesus brings the lesson home for our Pharisees.

Study Guide: 3) What Do You Want from Me?

Introduction: Have you ever asked God this question? Have a deeper discussion on what God wants from us.

The rich young ruler (Matthew 19:16–22)

The Jews on Pentecost (Acts 2:37)

Point 1. What is conflict management? Discuss.

Often people ask the right question but for the wrong reason. So how do we get the Creator's point of view?

Point 2. Blessings cost

Activity on the parable of the wedding feast: Three volunteers will fill the roles of the "chosen" that have been invited to attend your son's wedding this coming Saturday. Throw out the invitation, and see by a show of hands who will be coming. Find responses that sum up the three excuses: "I have new property," "I've invested in new equipment/work," and "I have personal things going on within my family." Now that you have your volunteers, let them build their cases with detail so the cases seem real. Now read Luke 14:16–24.

The question we need to ask to understand God's point of view is, "Who gave these people their gifts?" God did! We use blessings as an excuse, and then often we ask for more blessings.

Often we ask the question, "What do you want?" because we want something from God and are trying to figure out what the holdup is (more on that later). It seems we want to accept only answers that financially bless us.

We forget every blessing from God comes with a price tag. Discuss.

Point 3. How should we ask the question?

Listen to the question again. "What do you want from me?" People ask to find pity, not answers; to make God feel guilty for putting us in a situation; or just to blow off steam. The rich young ruler asked the question just so Christ would notice how well he was doing. God hears the question a lot, yet no one wants an answer, because they aren't asking a question. Instead they are making a statement. It's like when my wife ask me, "Do those clothes go there?" Believe me she isn't really looking for an answer. She is instead bringing something to my attention.

In Acts 2:37, how do the Jews ask? They ask in humbleness after realization of what they've done hits.

How do our children do this to us? Referring to the chapter "And in humility, once the "broken" process is complete, they finally open their ears, not to our voice as much as to their own demise.

Conclusion: "My Prayer" at the end of the chapter. When the focus comes off me and becomes about God (represented in the capitalization of *God* and the *i*), prayer begins to make sense.

Study Guide: 4) What's Stopping You?

Introduction: The introduction of this book makes a good introduction for this lesson. The next few studies will focus on the thought of "Seek and find."

Point 1. Following heart or Spirit

The story of Moses following his heart (Exodus 2:11–15)

The story of Moses following God (Exodus 3:1–10)

Extra information can be found in Hebrews 11:23–27.

Discuss the differences between a self-made path and holy ground.

I believe God has put passions within each of us. If you want to know what God wants from you, consider the passions you have. Be careful with specifics. It's the difference between I love fishing, and I love the outdoors. One take on the passions leads us to the lake instead of church.

Point 2. The path

You can take your pick of stories in scripture, and almost all of them show God's path isn't in our playbook. The story of Joshua and the walls of Jericho is an excellent example.-We may ask if the wrong path is necessarily a sinful one or if God brings us full circle.

The path you take to reach the goals is different. What path would you have come up with if we were the war counsel of Israel and Jericho lay before us? How do we take the wall? Was the parade option in our playbook?

God's path usually gets the "you have to be joking" response. Acts 2:43 describes Christians in awe of God as well, something that overshadows all other emotions.

It won't be a path you design—not to begin with, that is. Now, once God puts you where you need to be, we begin to develop ideas and work out issues, of course.

Point 3. Activity

Present two images to the class. One looks similar to a circle, but the ends don't meet. The other is like a square, but the ends on that last corner pass each other, making a small right angle. The class is given paper and told to draw the images before them. They draw a circle and a square. The lesson here is that the students assumed you meant to draw the shapes the way they felt you should have drawn them. Often we assume God is off a bit on His presentation of the path, and we just shake our heads and take our own.

Conclusion: Now, one may reason, "Why does the path taken matter, as long as we reach the destination?"

In response I would ask, "Does the path lead to the same destination?" I will refer back to my story and Moses. One often leads to self-righteousness, while the other leads to His righteousness.

People often ask why God doesn't bless them with an easier path. They even claim financial blessings would benefit the church. God isn't worried so much about what we do with blessings, but rather who we become as a result of those blessings.

Study Guide: 5) Here ... You Try

Introduction: Why does God remain silent at times? If you like movie clips, a fun one to use would by *Pirates of the Caribbean*.

The first time Jack Sparrow and Will Turner enter the cave at the Isla de Muerta Jack tells Will, "Not yet; wait for the opportune moment." Turner cannot wait and takes matters into his own hands. Then watch the scene near the end of the movie where Sparrow has returned to the Isla de Muerta one last time, to confront Barbossa. He offers a truce as he swipes a piece of the Aztec gold from the chest. "Not yet; wait to lift the curse until the opportune moment." As Jack finishes that statement, he directs it to Will.

Point 1. Test

Does God work in this manner? Refer to John 6:1–9. Note people want to continue to the miracle but miss verse 6.

Verses 5–6. People always jump to the miracle and overlook the test. The miracle is powerful, but the test is practical.

Step into the shoes of Philip. Where does he look first?

Point 2. Solutions

Where do we look for solutions? A huge utility/hospital bill hits, and you wonder what? It seems to be human nature to turn first to ourselves.

Next we may look to others for help. Only after we have exhausted our resources do we look to God. And often we look at him in anger asking why He did this.

Corrie Ten Boom quote: "Is God your steering wheel or your spare tire?"

Point 3. The opportune moment

Why does God do this? To answer this question you must ask another one. How often do we want to know He is there with us?

God's desire is for us to know He hears us. The bind we put Him in is simple. If prayers are answered too fast or easily, humans credit themselves. If we have to wait, we act childish and give up. And often God has no opportune moment, because we take matters into our own hands.

Conclusion: Refer to Judges 7; the story of Gideon brings this lesson out again. We turn to ourselves and credit ourselves. God knows this, and so He takes human strength out of the picture.

The Lord said to Gideon, "The troops with you are too many for me to give the Midianites into their hand, Israel would only take the credit away from me, saying 'My own hand has delivered me.'"

Now you can insert the self-centered man who can't stand to wait. The chapter contains a script on what the story would have looked like—giving up and walking away before God could let us know He is with us. No wonder he chose a man hiding in a winepress and scared. Sometimes God had to humble an entire nation, not just an individual.

Do you think He would humble a nation like that today?

Study Guide: 6) Where Will You Meet the Stone?

Introduction: This class needs to begin with the "box" illustration at the beginning chapter six. You simply set cardboard box in the midst of your class.

Play the illustration up to the breaking point. When do we feel like God has asked too much? You may have to dig in more on this point. Sadly, many may not feel this call, because they have ignored it for so long, justifying they don't have time.

From our families? Personal time/weekends? Ministries?

Point 1. Choices before the box

Many choose to walk away from the box, aka stone. Why? Others choose to ignore the box and refuse to acknowledge it. Then some have chosen to step in. How does stepping in change everything?

Point 2. What is the breaking point?

Is it the point we become a Christian, or is it something else altogether?

Refer to Matthew 21:42–44. This passage is addressed to the Jews. They are already a saved people, but this new teaching, or Gospel, makes them turn away. John 6:60, 66–68

How do these 2 verses apply to us? Each of us begins a walk with Christ that is exciting. But after a while, the honeymoon phase ends and we are faced with the "spiritual battlefield."

Refer to John 13:6–9. Peter, an apostle, is told, "If you don't let me wash you, you have no part with Me." This occurred after Peter was a follower. This is a continual wash (I John 1:7).

Point 3. Walking away or the struggle

Sin has no power to pull me away from God's grace, but to say I can't leave claims I have no free will or choice anymore.

Why does Paul make this statement? See Romans 9:3.

God intends marriage to last a lifetime. He intends your covenant with Him to last as well. He accepts us for "better or worse" as long as we continue to walk with Him and wrestle against the flesh. As Romans puts it, we have no reason to fear the security of God's promise. We simply get up when we fall and push forward.

I like to use the illustration of children learning to walk. The father always picks them up. Then they become toddlers learning to run and breaking stuff. The father may scold them but still help them up. Then we have teenagers, falling hard while trying to work in the family business. The parent will continue to pick them up, "if they will allow us!" They may get angry at having to work and just quit. We are lost when we refuse to try anymore. Some people question if they were ever saved. I would present to you the prodigal son. He was a son before he left.

The "seek and find" lessons have been full of excitement and adventure. But as we approach the stone, new lessons are presented. "Be still and know I AM God."

Conclusion: Discuss Peter's life. The poem "The Nails" at the end of chapter 6 is a beautiful way to enter this discussion.

Study Guide:7) The Silence

Introduction: When we think of silence, what comes to mind? Playing Darius Rucker's "I Got Nothing" may help direct their minds to "hurt silence" instead of to when the kids leave the house and it's quiet. Either way, work toward the non-pleasant silences.

Point 1. Doubting God's role or our own

The story "God's going to take care of me" in chapter 7 helps prepare a twist when Abraham takes the other route of moving instead of staying still.

Abraham was promised a son by God. Then God is mostly silent for twenty-five years. He promised in Genesis 12:4–5 to make Abram's descendants into a great nation. Then in Genesis 21 at the age of one hundred, he sees that promise fulfilled. What happened in the middle?

Which is the harder path? Moving or waiting?

Point 2. How do we view silence?

Exodus 14:13–14 shows Moses standing tall on God's promise, but verse 15 shows him behind the scene nervous from silences.

Silence scares us because we often view it as abandonment.

How does God view it? As a teacher in a class, a parent letting a child experience a lesson so that when he or she explains why, the child understands.

Point 3. Is God ever completely silent?

Use the example of a child in the car seat crying to be held. The parents may not be able to hold the child, but they speak words of comfort. How is God like this?

Refer to Psalm 19:1.

If children fall while learning to ride a bike, should we always rush to their side and smother them with attention? Or does there come a time we simply speak some encouragement instead of comfort?

The Holy Spirit was sent to be a "Comforter." The Holy Spirit through inspired men gave us the Bible, aka the "Words of Life." How many hurt and yet refuse to take comfort in His words?

Consider the blessing of another day.

Conclusion: How does viewing silence as abandonment affect us?

Often people want to complain about their problems to friends. They want sympathy. They want justice. They want someone on their side. But how does that help us move forward past the problem?

Sometimes we approach God this way when we seek his comfort. We walk beside Him pointing out the burdens we are carrying and demand that something be done. No relief can be given, because nothing has been let go.

Study Guide: 8) Be Still...

Introduction: Be still is a command given over and over in scripture to the "believer," not the "sinner." Why? These lessons help growth. A birth is needed before 'growth' can take place.

If you are hoping to grow spiritually, you will face these moments. The biggest on the list of lessons to look for is "Trust God over yourself."

Point 1. The wisdom of fools (I Corinthians 1:25) -King Saul

I Samuel 13, 15, and 17 are tied together in Saul's experiences with silence. Review these steps taken by Saul, and try to enter his shoes. In I Samuel 13 he was king and people looked to him for answers. What did silence do to his mind-set?

In I Sam 13:12, "I am king, and someone needs to do something."

In I Sam 15:15, "During the victory celebration, we will finish the command '*to kill everything*' as we offer sacrifices to God. I can make God's commandment better!"

In I Samuel 17 Saul stands before Goliath afraid to move. Samuel is not there, but he doesn't dare take matters into his own hands. And he doesn't try to make anything better. He simply sits waiting for something for forty days. Ultimately it seems God uses all this to open the door for David. Instead of Saul grasping this possibility, he chooses to become jealous of David.

Point 2. A miracle magnified -Lazarus

John 11:5–6. These verses don't seem to fit together, do they? In God's overall plan they do.

Read John11:17. We see at least six days have passed since Jesus was notified of Lazarus's condition. They experienced the illness, funeral, and mourning process while God remained silent.

Why does this miracle stand out to us? Because of the element God challenges. God takes on death!

God uses silence to set the stage for something more than another miracle showing powers over this physical world. He shows power beyond it!

Point 3. -The old prophet

Read Kings 13.

After reading the story, discuss the group's reaction to the young prophet and then the older one.

Why did the younger prophet trust the old one? He probably knew him; this was a man who had been used by God in the past.

Why did the old prophet lie? He knew how God's presence felt. He longed for that mountaintop experience again. God's voice had become silent in his life, and it seems he wanted to push his way back in.

Conclusion: All three of these accounts are about people who knew God's presence. They were all believers, and each story shows how believers handle silence. How do we react when we are told to be still? Learning to see the times of silence as times of preparation and begin using that time instead of wasting it is the key lesson. Sometimes God is waiting on others to lift up (David). Sometimes he plans to put emphasis on a point He is making (Lazarus). Sometimes we simply must be still (old prophet).

Study Guide: 9) ...And Know that I Am God

Introduction: Read Psalm 46:10. What thoughts come to mind? Many draw a picture of the serene. Gardens and mountaintops are often used in the artwork that embraces the passage. However, when we read the chapter, we realize that the passage was penned in a storm. This lesson will focus in how to endure the silence.

Point 1. Activity: the fairy tale

A lighter way of opening up this discussion is to ask the class to share their favorite Disney fairy tale. Now, most will be extremely easy to take and make this point. It's funny everyone wants the fairy tale, but forgets each fairy tale begins with tragedy that they are forced to endure. Cinderella's ball is meaningless without the rest of the story.

Point 2. Luke 7:18–23

John the Baptist asked the same questions that we do. Why is this happening? Why aren't you helping? What purpose could this possibly serve in Your will? Why are you silent? John is forced to sit in a prison cell and go over all the questions that silence brings, and finally he asks Jesus for answers.

What kind of answer is given? I'm taking care of everyone else right now, so wait your turn? Don't ask questions you know the answer to? I believe instead Jesus tells John to be still and know that He is the Christ. He offers up all the evidence of who He is and then tells John not to be offended because of how things are playing out. The answer John received was not the one he wanted, but it was an answer. God came to save the soul, not the body. His fight was bigger than John.

Understanding that God hears and answers is important. This makes the difference between *knowing God hears me and has addressed me,* and *feeling unheard and abandoned.*

Point 3. Faith makes the difference in how we see things

Our limited knowledge, plus our overabundant curiosity, make faith a *must*! You can take this thought and approach almost any story in scripture. I use Adam and Eve. Satan lies, we are super-curious, but we lack the knowledge and understanding to make a smart choice. Do we trust God or learn the hard way?

I skipped a great point in a previous chapter that fits well here. When we have to wait, often we just twiddle our thumbs and waste time. We should see these times of endurance as times of preparation. Often we don't want to wait or endure anything, because we want to move to the next chapter. I feel like I'm ready for what's next, and I don't even know what's coming!

Conclusion: The closing thoughts from Isaiah 40:30–31

The illustration God gives of lifting us up on the wings of an eagle is spot-on. Often God does not remove storms, but He strengthens us to rise above them.

Study Guide: 10) The Fire

Introduction: Read the first part of the chapter as a creative way to help people reenter this story without knowing which story they are in. This process helps us enter the "shoes" of Shadrach, Meshach, and Abednego. Discuss the faith factor that these young men had while God remained silent. One brutal detail that I left out of the chapter was a common practice used during this time and culture. It is very likely that these boys were made eunuchs upon their arrival. Consider that as you try to enter their mindset in staying commitment to God; they understood God's role.

Point 1. Seeing God in the smallest blessings

How could they have seen their story? Where else could they give credit? Where could they have given blame? Do we do this?

Understanding God's involvement and knowing He is in control are huge foundational needs before the storms hit their full strength.

Point 2. Why let them be thrown in?

What lessons do we take from this? I believe their answers to the king show an amazing clarity in the midst of chaos. Christians have made statements concerning peace and clarity of mind when horrific things happen ... like a plane going down or in the midst of other life-threatening experiences.

Point 3. Activity

Shadrach, Meshach, and Abednego knew God was with them by noticing small blessings. They knew that God was sustaining them. Since this chapter was more creative writing, maybe your class will share some struggles they are facing and then note small blessings in the midst of those trials. People love to share the ways they see God in their storms.

Conclusion: **God understands when we push, in prayer.**

I shared the story about my friend Terry. I used this story to bring a different kind of struggle to the discussion. In his situation the choice to move forward in prayer with trying to have children was not a lack of faith. It wasn't wrong. Sometimes the choices don't boil down to a wrong way or a right way. They simply boil down to us pushing forward in prayer, in the only ways we know how. The problem areas are how we take the answer no or not yet.

Extra Material (*The Storm* was written by a friend and mother whose eighteen-month-old daughter was stricken with severe seizures for days)

The Storm

A fierce storm is raging about you, and you fear there is nothing to do. There is a place in your heart where He meets you; and in the eye of the storm He carries you through.

Don't let go or leave the eye, or the storm will take you in. Nothing will overtake you while you are holding on to Him.

There is a place of peace and rest, safe from the battles of life. Though the mighty waves crash around you, here you're safe from turmoil and strife.

For the Lord never sleeps nor slumbers while His children are in pain. He alone has the power to sustain you until you are whole again.

Oh, please lean ever closer to Him and just hold on tight. Looking through the dark waves, beyond you will see the Great Healer, Redeemer, the Light.

—Donna S. Dungan

Study Guide: 11) Untouchable

This class centers around why the world must see Christians suffer.

Introduction: Open a discussion on requests we bring to God. A list of request you may want to use can be found in chapter 11. You may present these with power point to the class and refer to them later.

Many prayers have a universal theme—I don't want to hurt or be vulnerable.

Point 1. Does God want us to become untouchable?

Often we quote verses like Psalm 55:22, Matthew 11:28–30, or I Peter 5:7 to show God's intent to free us from all these burdens. God never says, "Cast your burdens on me, and I will take them." This is a worldly view of becoming untouchable. Go back and reread these verses in their context, because some may want to argue this point. The promise is to sustain us and strengthen us to handle them. "Rest" and "freeing us" from burdens are very different thoughts.

Here are verses that show us how God intends for us to become untouchable: John 16:33, Matthew 10:28

Point 2. Back to the fire

Revisit the story of the fiery furnace one last time. Why didn't God stop the king before the fire? Why didn't he stop the men? Why not blow out the flames? In this story, God takes on the real threat.

Refer to John 10:28.

Our view must become more like God's. It's not the body he makes untouchable; it's the soul.

Point 3. From the world's view

The world takes note of suffering. It's the only thing that breaks down barriers and helps people to connect. It is a universal language.

Before the furnace everyone in the kingdom feared the fire, except Shadrach, Meshach, and Abednego. They feared God. After they walked out of the furnace, everyone else realized who was to be feared.

> **The fear of the LORD is the beginning of wisdom, And the knowledge of the Holy One is understanding.**
> **—Proverbs 9:10**

What does it mean to be holy? Set apart? Is it a divine plan of protection from pain? Or is "being holy" allowing our light to shine before humanity?

Conclusion: Prayers of surrender. What do you suppose that term means? Take the prayers you opened the class with and discuss how they might change or evolve into more.

Why must we learn to pray like this? Go back to those original prayers you listed for the class and deepen the thoughts. Examples are in the chapter.

Study Guide: 12) After the Fire

This lesson focuses more on what happens to us if we don't suffer.

Introduction: People come to God for a refuge, a safe place. They want to become Untouchable as we discussed last week.

Refer to II Corinthians 12:7–8, Paul's "thorn in the flesh."

So we come to Him and cast our burdens on Him, and He hands them back to us? How can God be a refuge but allow us to be tormented?

Paul describes his thorn as "in the flesh." He acknowledges that the "earthly burden" doesn't necessarily make it a "spiritual" one. How do thorns mold the soul?

Point 1. When are we pulled away from Him?

King David is probably the most-favored character in the Old Testament, yet what were his sins? Now can you tell me which sins are before 2 Samuel 11, and which came after? What changed?

As long as David was under pressure and persecution, he was a spiritual giant, but as soon as God gives him peace, what happens? Compare David to Uriah as David observes his steadfast passion and willingness to suffer with the armies of God. Again in I Chronicles 20 and 21, David goes from giant-killing, to peace, to sin.

Point 2. Is there a happily ever after on earth?

Our topic is "After the Fire," what comes next? Is there a point where God will give us a Utopia on this side of the grave?

Solomon was given that. What happened to him? His wisdom and riches are evident, but I don't see his name referenced in Hebrews 11 and other passages that talk about spiritual giants. Utopias destroy the spiritual side of people.

There will always be another fire on the horizon.

Point 3. Poor advice

So what do we do when we have to rest? Many give others the advice to vacation and give in. Work harder so you don't have time to think about it. Get more involved at church to put things in perspective. Study more, and become stronger than it.

Refer to Ecclesiastes 12:12.

Study is a wonderful way to draw peace, but sometimes when everything is crashing down, I don't have the strength to run to Him. So we learn to call on Him, and He runs to us. We learn to cry in His arms.

Conclusion: In John 13 Christ washes the apostles' feet. Often we aren't comfortable coming before Him in this avenue. We prefer approaching Him in times we are strong. I'm ready, Lord. I will not fail you today. We desire his approval like children who hope their parents notice when they perform well.

Embrace this other role God plays—as physician, healer, shepherd. We are strengthened within the fires, and between them we take rest in His arms. The blacksmith holds the sword in the fires while He shapes it. He then holds the weapon in the waters to cool it, so that it becomes strong again in the shape He desired.

Study Guide: 13) Our Ultimate Example

This class can be done in many ways. For longer class periods, you may want to include each of these closing thoughts with each original lesson. In a normal quarter, you have thirteen sessions to fill. If you choose to cover this lesson by mixing it along the way, the closing thoughts can be used as a final class.

You could also easily present this class as a two-part series if you prefer to combine two previous chapters.

Regardless of how and when you present it, make sure you include these powerful points, which bring clarity to every other point in the study. They serve as a divine exclamation point to the book.

Introduction: Depending on the way you approach your series (breaking class 13 up through the study or making it one class at the end), you still need to begin with this verse.

> For we do not have a high priest who cannot sympathize with our weaknesses, but One who has been tempted in all things as we are, yet without sin.
> —Hebrews 4:15

1-The Question; The Beginning

Genesis 1:1–3, 9–10

Who is God? God's version of the question would have been, "Who AM I?" And from the very beginning, He answers the question. As He designed the world (including Golgotha), He designed His role in our lives. He has been true to that role ever since. Two thousand years ago God sent His Son into the world. And His name shall be

Immanuel, which translates to "God with us." This name tells us who He is and why He came.

2-Seeking Answers; The Birth

John 1:14, -I John 5:13

God dwells among us. He came seeking to give answers.

3-What Do You Want from Me? His Life and Ministry

John 7:16–18, John 14:8–10

This doesn't mean that Christ never thought about the options the world offered. He was tempted just as we are, yet Jesus refrained because He chose to mirror God's will, making the Father's plan one with His own.

4-What's Stopping You? Entering Jerusalem

-John 12:12 through John 13:1-4

As He enters Jerusalem, so many 'fiery furnaces' are being cranked up before Him, but nothing stopped Christ. Why? Christ knew who God was, and He knew who He Himself was. He understood the Father's will and accepted it.

5-Here ... You Try. The Upper Room to Gethsemane

John 13:5 and all that takes place through Matthew 26:36–37

Does God understand how we feel when more is asked of us than we could possible give? He understands! And in those moments when

Christ pours all of His strength out for His followers, and still God requires more from Him, He turns to God for strength in prayer.

6-Where Will You Meet The Stone? The Garden

Matthew 26:38–46

Here in the garden Christ chooses to fall upon the stone and become broken to God's will rather than His own. He understands how it feels to break upon the stone!

7-The Silence; Mock Trial

Matthew 26:59–64

The self-righteous religious leader of the day will call forth witness after witness to twist the truth, and no one will speak on behalf of Christ. Through all of this Jesus will hear silence from the heavens.

8-Be Still; Before Pilate

John 18:37–38

Everything that the Jews and Romans are putting on Him makes a mockery of God. In the same instance everything being carried out prepares Christ to become the sacrificial Lamb.

9-And Know I AM God; Through the Scourging

John 19:1–4

Please realize, they are both still as they endure the scourging; One endures the experiences, and One endures having to watch. And both stay true to the course of action, because they both know God's plan and God's will. They understand!

10-The Fire; The Crucifixion

Philippians 2:1–8

He knows what worldly "fires" are. He endured them for thirty-three-plus years.

11- Untouchable

John 3:16

What more could He have given to you to show He cares and understands? He suffered and died so that this point is untouchable.

12-After the Fire

II Timothy 4:7–8

Christ simply went from one set of problems to the next. Never did he find an earthly peace. And when His strength was spent, He didn't study more or work harder. He simply found moments of heavenly peace in prayer before His Father, between the fires.

References

I have listed references by chapter and the order in which they are used. Example (7:1) is chapter 7, first reference listed.

1   1:1 Online Parallel Bible Project. 2004–16. Online study aid, http://biblehub.com/text/genesis/3-5.htm.

2   2:1 Lucado, Max, *A Gentle Thunder*, Word Publishing, 1995, p. 21.
    2:2 Evidence for God (website). "Little Old Lady and the Atheist," www.godandscience.org/humor/lady.html.

5   5:1 Lucado, Max, *A Gentle Thunder*, Word Publishing, 1995, pp. 90–91.
    5:2 Wyatt, Ron. Revealing God's Treasure. Crossing the Red Sea video, http://www.arkdiscovery.com/red_sea_crossing.htm.

7   7:1 http://www.dailymotion.com/video/xxi51j_jerry-clower-god-s-gonna-take-care-of-me_fun

9   9:1 Dr. Myles Monroe, 7 Principles of an Eagle Kwee Lain, August 22, 2007, https://sharelife.wordpress.com/2007/08/22/7-principles-of-an-eagle-dr-myles-monroe/.

12 12:1 Source was observed on the sporting field at GCBC when cabin 8 boys from the Hattiesburg week were shamed in Ultimate Frisbee by the old guy. You know who you are. :)

About the Author

Byron Smith has worked in several ministries over the last 20 years. After receiving his BA in Biblical Studies through Faulkner University, he served as youth minister, Inner-city evangelist, and presently the Director of Gulf Coast Bible Camp. Throughout all these works, He has primarily been tied to youth and their families.

"I am not a preacher, but I often speak from the pulpit. I am not a counselor, yet I spend endless hours counseling young people. I am not a fund-raiser and still I have been responsible for raising funds for a Bible Camp the past ten years. I am not a plumber, lumber-jack, or a list of other titles and yet I find myself doing that work as well.

I am a student of God's word, who is not afraid to ask questions and learn. And because I seek to dwell in His presence, He has made me successful in everything I have attempted to do. And so I decided to put Him to the ultimate test and write a book :)

Over the years, I have hurt with a lot of people who have struggled to hear God. Because I suffer from the human condition, I have had my share of trials as well. This book is my gift to Him and I pray that He uses it as He sees fit. May God receive all the glory, honor, and praise that it can produce."

Printed in the United States
By Bookmasters